KT-471-547

Criminal Justice
and Related Services
for Young
Adult Offenders

A Review

CITY COLLEGE NORWICH
LIBRARY SERVICES

LEARNING
SUPPORT
SERVICES

Please return
on or before
the last date
stamped below

and Related Services
for Young
Adult Offenders

A Review

Stewart Asquith
Centre for the Study of the Child & Society
University of Glasgow

Elaine Samuel
Centre for Social Welfare Research
University of Edinburgh

THE SCOTTISH OFFICE
CENTRAL RESEARCH UNIT

NORWICH CITY COLLEGE LIBRARY

Stock No	187399	
Class	364. 36 ASQ	
Cat.		Proc.	

EDINBURGH: HMSO

187 399

© Crown copyright 1994
First published 1994

Applications for reproduction should be made to HMSO

ISBN 0 11 495243 4

The views expressed in this report are those of the authors alone and do not necessarily
represent those of The Scottish Office Home and Health Department or the
Secretary of State for Scotland.

Contents

Acknowledgements

This study was made possible by financial support from the The Scottish Office Home and Health Department.

A number of practitioners, policy makers and members of voluntary organisations gave of their time to be interviewed for the project and we would like to take the opportunity here to thank them.

Particular thanks are due to Dr Joe Curran, Principal Research Officer in the Central Research Unit's Criminological Research Branch at the The Scottish Office who assisted us throughout the project. Fiona Hird of the Civil and Criminal Justice Statistics Unit is to be thanked for not only making available unpublished data for use in Elaine Samuel's report but also for her considerable interest in the project and her comments on the draft of the Gender Issues report.

This review encapsulates the situation of Young Offenders and Special Projects at one particular time. It is a dynamic field which changes rapidly. Some of the projects and approaches described here will have ceased to exist before publication of this report, others emerge. We hope that this 'snapshot' will help place the thinking on Young Offenders in the 1990s in context.

Notwithstanding the debt we owe to those mentioned and to others who helped in the production of this volume, responsibility for interpretation and for any mistakes is ours alone.

Stewart Asquith
University of Glasgow

Elaine Samuel
University of Edinburgh

Part 1

A Review of Criminal Justice and Related Issues for Young Adult Offenders

Stewart Asquith and Elaine Samuel

Chapter One

Background to the Research

Main Objectives of the Review

This project takes the form of a preliminary review of the measures available for and the issues associated with young adult offenders. Within the restrictions of what was a six month project, it is impossible to give a detailed overview of all measures that are available for young adult offenders. In the interests of economy, four main objectives were identified for the review, as follows:

(a) To identify key issues and areas of concern in relation to young adult offenders (for the purposes of this project defined as those between 16 and 21).

(b) To identify the range of measures and initiatives available for young offenders at the various stages of the criminal justice process.

(c) To review relevant literature and research findings relating to strategies for dealing with young offenders, particularly those designed to divert young people from criminal and disruptive behaviour and to divert them from key stages such as prosecution, sentencing and custody.

(d) To identify key policy and practice issues arising from the review which may form the basis for future empirical research.

Scotland, England and Wales constituted the main focus of our inquiries but, because of recent developments in Europe in the criminal justice field, information was also collected on European initiatives. Reference is also made in the report to some of the key differences in the legislative frameworks between European countries and how these impinge on the availability of measures for the group which constitutes the focus of our investigation - young adult offenders.

Main Sources of Data

Data were collected from a variety of sources in order to provide as wide a coverage as possible of information on measures for young adult offenders. The main sources included:

(i) a review of relevant research and related literature;

(ii) interviews with key personnel with a direct interest in young adult offenders. These can be divided broadly into four main groups-

Members of voluntary agencies such as APEX, National Children's Homes, NACRO, SACRO etc.;

Members of criminal justice systems and statutory agencies, particularly social work;

Policy makers, including the member of the cabinet at the French Ministry of Justice responsible for developing a programme of social crime prevention; and Researchers.

(iii) information sought from most European countries on the availability of measures for young adult offenders (by means of a small postal survey).

In addition, we also attended a number of interdisciplinary conferences and workshops on services for young offenders with audiences reflecting the whole spectrum of personnel concerned directly with young adult offenders, including sheriffs, prison officers, police, teachers, Children's Panel members, project leaders and policy makers.

Moreover, the diversity of individuals and agencies we felt obliged to contact reflects the increasing trend to search for measures for dealing with a particularly vulnerable section of the population without relying exclusively on the resources within the criminal justice system.

Background to the Research

(i)   Young Adult Offenders and the use of Custody.

The problems associated with young adult offenders cannot be seen in isolation from the population of offenders as a whole nor the experiences of young people generally.

In relation to the latter, it is generally recognised that young people are at a particularly vulnerable stage in the life cycle with the transition from school to work, the difficulty of locating themselves in the labour market and the attempt to establish a life independent from their families. Because of the changes society undergoes, the criminal justice system has also to adapt and modify its practices and, as Spencer noted some time ago,

"We must continually remind ourselves that criminal law and corrections is only one of society's ways of maintaining social control." (Spencer 1973).

These present serious challenges to young people at the best of times but at a time of economic constraint and with ideological changes and their implications for social policies, particularly social security, unemployment, housing and education, the young have found themselves even more vulnerable and marginalised. Nor is this a British phenomenon for comment has been made on the increasing marginalisation of the young and their exclusion from mainstream society elsewhere in Europe (see Bailleau and Garioud 1990; Whitehead et al. 1991). The implication is that any attempt to reduce crime amongst the young will have to take into consideration the social and economic circumstances in which they find themselves. And as we shall see, recent trends in crime prevention have been moving in the direction of a closer relationship with social policy and a move away from purely individualistic notions of crime causation.

As for the criminal justice system, any analysis of the situation of young adults has to be seen in the context of rising crime rates, the crisis in the prison system in trying to cope with increasing numbers of offenders, the search for alternatives to custody and a general reconceptualisation of crime control and its objectives. We will return to these issues later, not simply because they provide the background against which the search for measures for young adults has to be appraised but rather because the search for alternative means of dealing with young adults is part of a wider attempt to devise new means for dealing with offenders, not just in the UK but more widely in the political arena.

In seeking to evaluate measures for young adult offenders, as we shall discuss more fully later, it has to be recognised that there may well be a number of competing objectives which have to be taken into consideration. That is, as well as the aim of reducing crime, measures may well be assessed in terms of how far they achieve other ends such as the reduction of the prison population, fiscal savings, the reduction of fear and the promotion of security. The search for alternatives to custody can only be adequately understood with reference to the pragmatic concerns associated with custody (see Bailleau and Garioud 1990).

(ii)   Crime and the Search for Community Based Programmes.

In the UK the recognition of the need to develop alternatives to custody was expressed most clearly in 1988 in the Green Paper Punishment, Custody and the Community (1988) and the 1990 White Paper Crime, Justice and Protecting the Public.

The Green Paper and the White Paper had crystallised thinking on approaches to dealing with offenders generally and were premised on a number of considerations in common with other documents which had appeared throughout the decade. These were that:

alternatives for young adult offenders should be sought drawing on the experience of developments in the juvenile field;

custody is often inappropriate and can be counterproductive;

the community is a more appropriate site for penal practice;

existing community based programmes could be extended in range and availability;

punishment for offensive behaviour is appropriate;

better interagency co-operation is required to improve service provision.

3

What developments in Britain illustrated was what Farrell and Heidensohn (1991) referred to as the **twin track** approach in which developments in community initiatives were made in association with the principle that offenders had to recognise their offence, and accept both responsibility for it and the punishment. Shifting ideologies of crime and punishment went hand in hand very neatly with the pragmatic concern to reduce the prison population.

Young adult offenders had been clearly identified as a group for particular attention and in 1988 the Home Office Action Plan required every probation authority in England and Wales to draw up a strategy for young adult offenders. What the Green Paper, the Home Office Action Plan and the White Paper all had in common was the importance attached to the development of measures within the community within a framework of co-ordinated local strategies. Throughout the 80's the philosophy of interagency co-operation was manifested in the growth of a number of multi-disciplinary organisations including: Action on Youth Crime, NAJC, Out of Court, Scottish Forum and Crime Concern.

In Scotland, two recent developments in particular have implications for the development of community based alternatives for young adult offenders and also will be followed up later in the review. These are the 100% funding strategy and the establishment of National Objectives and Standards for Social Work Services in the Criminal Justice System (1991).

Concern to reduce the prison populations of European countries is well documented (Feest 1988,1990; and Bailleau and Garioud 1990) and the population of young adults in prison has come in for particular focus (Baechtold 1988). Baechtold (1988) in particular urges us to treat young adult offenders not as a fringe but as the main group in both the criminal justice and prison systems requiring specific attention. Given that they constitute the largest age category, broadly defined, there has to be some surprise at the fact that there is a distinct shortage of both resources and alternative measures for this group of offenders.

Nevertheless, developments over the past decade or so have generally pointed to the need to deal with more offenders in the community with reference being made to the specific needs of young adult offenders in the 16 -21 age group.

Bailleau and Garioud (1990) have identified five main factors which can be used to account for the increasing commitment to the development of community based measures. These are the substantial rise in petty crime; the growth of privatised protection systems; economic crisis and its effect on the young; the crisis in social work; and the crisis in the criminal justice system.

What Bailleau and Garioud (1990) and others (Farrel and Heidensohn 1991; Feest 1988, 1990; Graham 1990) assert on the basis of these is that the criminal justice system itself can be seen to have limited effect in controlling crime and that the search for alternative means for dealing with offenders has shifted outwith the criminal justice system for both pragmatic and ideological reasons. The acceptance of extra-judicial means for dealing with offenders has been accompanied by the acceptance that criminal policy may have to be formulated in conjunction with social and public policies. Reducing the prison population and the volume of cases which the criminal justice system processes may only be achieved by the adoption of alternative measures alien to traditional conceptions of criminal justice and in which the very social and economic conditions seen to contribute to crime are tackled.

The implication of all this is that at a time in which there is obvious fundamental rethinking of how offence behaviour may be dealt with, there is a lack of clarity as to the objectives and purposes set by new measures designed to reduce crime and prison populations. We will return to this, but the main point to be made here is that the very pragmatic concern to reduce both criminal justice and prison populations has itself contributed to a radical rethinking about the nature of crime, its causes and how to deal with it.

(iii)   Reductionist Strategies.

Changes and developments in criminal justice have increasingly become influenced by the principles of diversion, decriminalisation, de-institutionalisation and crime prevention. (Bailleau and Garioud 1990, Feest 1988, 1990). Feest (1990) has outlined the variety of forms of what he refers to as **reductionist strategies** (by which he means those measures designed to reduce the prison and criminal justice populations) employed in Europe and which will provide a useful framework for our review.

Reductionist strategies can be categorised in a number of ways and these include:

(a)   **Entry Avoidance**
Examples of entry avoidance include informal cautioning of offenders, mediation between victims and offenders and general diversion of offenders away from formal processes of social control.

(b)   **Process Interruption**
Again, this includes unconditional dismissals (police cautions etc.); conditional dismissals (payment of a fine, restitution, victim offender reconciliation); the handling of cases by agencies outwith the criminal justice system; the diversion of complainants and victims.

(c)   **Remand Avoidance**
By this he refers to the various bail projects that are available, mainly in the UK.

(d)   **Conviction/Sentencing Avoidance**
Conviction avoidance can take the form of informal settlements or referral to a mediation agency as can sentencing avoidance which also refers to the use of the deferred sentence.

(e)   **Imprisonment Avoidance**

Examples of imprisonment avoidance include community service orders; non carrying out of prison sentences (e.g. on sentences of up to four months); temporary release; early release, etc.

What this outline illustrates is that the attempt to reduce the prison population and the criminal justice population involves all stages of the criminal justice process. Any analysis of the crisis apparent in most western systems of criminal justice has to be based on an understanding of the integrity of the criminal justice system as a whole. What Feest has omitted from his framework is the general commitment to preventive strategies and the significance these now have in the development of measures to reduce offence behaviour and ultimately the prison population. In that respect, Feest's outline has to be supplemented by reference to the analyses of preventive measures as discussed by Graham (1990) and Bailleau and Garioud (1990).

(iv)   **Young Adult Offenders.**

The comments above have largely referred to reductionist and community based strategies for offenders in general. Our concern is with measures available for young adult offenders. Nevertheless, for the purposes of this review we have decided to examine some of the measures and strategies available for juvenile offenders as well as for young adult offenders for a number of reasons.

First, it is by no means unambiguous just who is a young adult offender, since the juvenile justice systems of both Scotland and England and Wales have jurisdiction over young people who may be dealt with by the adult criminal justice system or the juvenile justice system. In Scotland, criminal law allows that 16 or 17 year olds may be dealt with both in the Children's Hearings and in the criminal justice system. The Council of Europe crime statistics reveal clearly the difficulty of drawing parallels between countries which employ very different age classification schemes. Given that the peak offending ages straddle the age classifications employed in the UK systems of juvenile and criminal justice, to exclude a consideration of some of the developments for younger offenders would be a serious omission.

Secondly, there have been suggestions made in both Scotland (Child Care Law Review 1990) and England and Wales (Crime Justice and Protecting the Public 1990) that the age of jurisdiction for the respective juvenile justice systems should be increased to accommodate more of the older age range of young offenders within the ambit of juvenile justice.

Thirdly, any cursory glance at the variety of age categories and classifications employed throughout Europe reveals wide diversity of the age at which young people may be dealt with in either the juvenile or adult criminal justice system (Dunkel 1991). For example, in Germany all young people up to the age of 18 will be dealt with in the juvenile system and those up to 21 may be so dealt with (Feest 1988) with no special category of young adult offenders being recognised. In Finland, 18 and 19 year olds will be dealt with in a juvenile court (Joutsen 1991) and in Belgium the age of criminal responsibility is 18 (Walgrave et al. 1991). Many countries in fact claim that they have no specific category of young adults (Walgrave 1991; Feest, interview 1991).

Dunkel (1991) presents a detailed statement of the basic legal differences between countries in Europe as regards both the age of criminal responsibility and the age of majority. Despite the variety in age classification of offenders throughout Europe (including both Scotland and England and Wales in his analysis) he identifies a number of commonalities between systems of juvenile justice that are pertinent to our review. Throughout Europe, there is a movement to raise the age at which young people may be dealt with within juvenile justice systems and removed from the ambit of the criminal court. Likewise, the concern to reduce prison populations and the use of custody in general has seen the development of a wealth of diversionary and preventive measures for both juveniles and adults, some of which straddle both juvenile and criminal justice systems. The measure which has gained increasing favour in Europe for young offenders has taken the form of mediation and reconciliation programmes.

Fourthly, and here the European data has been particularly helpful, whereas there may be crucial differences between the legal systems in Europe in terms of age classification, it is clear that whatever age is set, the interface between juvenile justice and criminal justice systems presents transitional problems in all systems. The Scottish system, however, poses particularly severe transitional problems for young people because of the fundamental differences between the welfare philosophy of the Children's Hearing system and the rather more severe approach of the criminal justice system as it applies to adults.

Fifthly, and related to the last point directly, many of the measures adopted for juveniles and children have been seen to have had a dramatic effect in reducing the number of children in custody or in institutions. A number of commentators have argued that the lessons learnt in relation to the younger offenders have to be applied, or at least considered, for the older age groups. Programmes which have been considered to have been successful have been replicated or advocated as appropriate for the older offender. For example, in a research report to the Home Office Research and Planning Unit, Evans and Wilkinson (1990) confirm one of the main objectives of the review they undertook in Northampton as being:

"To consider whether the type of strategies which are successful with juveniles in achieving diversion from court and from custody could be extended to young adult offenders" (p 1).

It is undoubtedly the case that in the past few years the implications of the diversionary schemes promoted for children and juveniles have become more acceptable for the older offender. The difficulty for our purposes is that this does not necessarily only apply to the young adult offender.

Lastly, many of the developments in Europe and elsewhere are of a preventive nature and are targeted not at any specific age group but are designed to deal with the social and economic conditions which are seen to lead to criminal activity. It is widely acknowledged that 16 - 21 year olds, who account for a large proportion of offending behaviour, are also the group most likely to experience some of the consequences of poverty, unemployment, poor housing and generally reduced opportunities. For that reason, measures aimed at the social and political conditions which are seen to contribute to criminal behaviour are not necessarily age specific. The social crime prevention programmes in France are an example.

For these reasons, reference will be made throughout the review to measures and programmes which apply to children and juveniles though the focus of our inquiry is the young adult offender. To omit references to programmes for younger offenders would, however, be to omit measures which are seen to have potential for young adults and for reducing criminal behaviour in general.

What follows has been divided into three main sections and will include:

Relevant Research;
Available Measures; and
Conclusions and Recommendations.

Chapter Two

Research Literature

As noted above, one of the difficulties encountered in the production of this review was in identifying measures and programmes exclusively devoted to the situation of young adult offenders. The ambiguities and relevance of age and the fact that many measures are seen to have general import for offenders and not just for specific categories has meant that this review is wide ranging. This however in no way militates against achieving the objectives of the review. If anything it is of considerable benefit.

Current Approaches

It is clear that though there is a commitment to diverting offenders from the criminal justice system and specifically from custody, there is an absence of clarity as to the main objectives and aims sought in the pursuit and implementation of community based measures and programmes. The "reductionist strategy" identified by Feest (1990) conceals a wide diversity of conflicting and often competing aims which may include punishment, welfare, protecting the community, community regeneration and so on. NACRO (1989) also attributes the ambiguity in purpose inherent in recent criminal policy developments as to an inevitable outcome of a piecemeal and pragmatic approach to the development of community based alternatives. This presents at least two problems.

One is that the lack of clarity in objectives for programmes for offenders may well mean that the way in which they are implemented is dependent less on a clear statement of principle and more on the assumptions and attitudes about dealing with offenders, or indeed about the programme itself, maintained by key personnel.

The other is that the research literature has generally concentrated on the effects of measures on offending behaviour and has tended to ignore other considerations in evaluating or monitoring measures.

There is a wealth of research material on measures for dealing with offenders (see McIvor 1990, Gottschalk 1987, Faugeron 1991, Bennett-Emslie et al. 1990) and we do not intend in the space of a short review to present detailed statements of their contents. Rather we have identified key themes and issues common to much of the literature, and though we have drawn widely by including literature on measures for offenders generally, the relevance of these commonalties to young adult offenders will be articulated in subsequent sections.

Quite apart from the contribution it could make to reducing the volume of cases going through the criminal justice system, the move to community based measures has been, in some senses, based on an act of faith. This is because the history of research into the efficacy of various non-custodial measures has been one in which there has been little reason for optimism about the merits of community based alternatives.

For the decade or more following its publication in 1974, Robert Martinson's thesis that 'nothing works' made a profound impact upon penal policy and practice and became "synonym for penal pessimism" (Mair 1991b). The power of Martinson's original claim was reinforced by a sequence of papers (see Lipton et al 1975; Brody 1976). By the late 80's and early 90's, however, it had partly given way to a new spirit of optimism. The history of research from the 'what works' perspective is one in which can be traced increasing confidence in the significance of community based measures to reduce offending as well as to reduce prison populations.

The position now adopted, as we shall see, is not that nothing works but that there is no universal solution to the problem of offending behaviour. Projects can work, if they follow a number of clear guidelines. For example, there is more likelihood of a reduction in reoffending if programmes are adapted to the needs or the offence behaviour of individuals (NACRO 1989; McIvor 1990). Also where measures are directed at specific behaviours or behavioural problems, there is more likelihood of success.

But what is clear is that there is less chance of reducing reoffending rates where custodial sentences are imposed. Since young adult offenders are proportionately more likely to be the subject of custodial sentences, then there is concern that current measures relating to young adults may well contribute to an increase rather than a reduction in the prison population (NACRO 1989).

These all find clear reflection in the research literature of the last decade - both in the reports of original research and in the quite substantial numbers of reviews of research literature (Gendreau and Ross 1987; McIvor 1990; Andrews and Kessling et al. 1980). What concerns us here are the main findings and underlying themes of the most recent research literature, particularly as it relates to young offenders. As a corpus of knowledge, it may itself be characterised as driven by the desire to find out 'what works'. Certainly, many of the main issues addressed by the literature can be understood in this light.

Criteria of Success

Martinson's thesis relies upon recidivism as the sole criterion of success of all penal disposals. Recent discussion and re-evaluation of this traditional measure of success is marked by dissatisfaction with its prime role in evaluation studies. This has been most clearly stated by Mair (1991b) who points to a number of ways in which recidivism may not be an appropriate way to measure the success or otherwise of penal measures.

Mair argues that it is unclear whether the indicators used to measure recidivism actually do so - acts of recidivism can only be measured in so far as they come to the notice of criminal justice agents.

Also, measures of recidivism lack precision, with little account being taken of the kinds of offences responsible for reconviction and the patterns of reconviction following the termination of differing disposals. Recidivist rates, moreover, rarely take account of the impact of policing practice upon the likelihood of apprehension, prosecution and reconviction.

As the sole criterion of success, recidivism takes no account of the differing aims and objectives of different penal disposals. For example, evaluation of high tariff probation programmes must also measure whether or not they are successful in recruiting those offenders most at risk of custody; evaluation of community service programmes must also measure whether they are successful in introducing an element of reparation, and so on. This requires that evaluation studies of penal disposals be preceded by a clear formulation and prioritization of the aims and objectives of the disposals under evaluation.

As we shall also see in the following chapter, criticisms of programmes for offenders have focused on the way in which their lack of a clear statement of principle has contributed to the failure of the programme quite apart from its intrinsic merits. The complex nature of sentencing and the differing multi-purpose nature of various penal disposals demands, then, that multi-dimensional measures be used to evaluate their success.

Disposals should also be evaluated by criteria which lie outside their primary penal aims but take into account their general viability. For example, the cost of a disposal against the cost of possible alternatives, the willingness of sentencers to use the disposal, and the views of the clients (offenders) themselves, all constitute crucial criteria by which disposals must be measured before it can be said whether or not they work. The relevance of Mair's analysis will be all the more apparent when we later consider some of the actual programmes in operation.

In response to the pessimism of the nothing works philosophy, the economic realities and political context in which measures are implemented are seen to inhibit the implementation of programmes which we know work but which are starved of funding and adequate resources. The shortage of resources for community based measures is attributed to the fact that resources continue to be directed to the prison system despite all the concerns expressed about it (see Curtis 1992, Sinclair 1992).

But what Mair has done is to mirror the approach taken by Feest in asserting that measures have to be evaluated not simply in terms of the effect on crime reduction but also in terms of how they fulfil other criteria such as reducing the prison population, reducing the caseload of an overcrowded criminal justice system, reducing expenditure and so on.

The Research Literature

Some of these concerns have, in fact, already been taken up in the research literature, particularly in the evaluations of new penal measures. Here, more than elsewhere, clarification of aims and objectives have generated criteria of success broader in scope than the single criterion of recidivism.

The Community Service Order, for example, has been evaluated in terms of its cost, its ability to realise secondary goals such as skill acquisition, perceptions and attitudes of sentencers and offenders, the quality of its placements, its diversionary functions and its net -widening effects (Pease et al. 1977; McIvor 1989; Carnie 1990).

Likewise, Intermediate Treatment (IT) in Scotland has recently been assessed by measuring not just the offending and troublesome behaviour of children but also the social functioning and esteem of children before and after their involvement, and the attitudes of children and their parents to IT (Bennett-Emslie et al. 1990). In the evaluation of IT in England and Wales, measures were employed such as the level of prosecution of 14-16 year olds, diversion from custody and use for ethnic minorities (NACRO, 1989).

The recent string of research reports on intensive probation schemes for young offenders in England and Wales all give a crucial role to their ability to divert young offenders from custodial sentences (Raynor 1988; Roberts 1989; Brownlee 1990). In doing so, sophisticated methods have been and continue to be developed in order to compare those sentenced to custody with those sentenced to the alternative disposal being evaluated. This has involved identifying those characteristics of young offenders and their offences which are likely to influence their tariff position.

In addition to diversionary efficacy, these intensive probation schemes have been evaluated in terms of their cost effectiveness in comparison with custody, their helpfulness to clients, their use for female and ethnic minority offenders as well as reconviction rates during and subsequent to the completion of the programme.

The development of mediation and reparation schemes, particularly in Europe, has also resulted in a number of research reports which serve to highlight the fact that offence behaviour has to be seen as only one amongst a number of criteria of success to be employed. Other considerations, such as victim satisfaction, the effect on the offender of the symbolic act of reparation, quite apart from the monetary or time value of involvement in the scheme, have all to be taken into account (Dunkell 1990; Pelikan 1990, 1991; Walgrave et al. 1991; Peyre 1990; Kimberly et al. 1991; Plewig 1990; Hessmer 1990).

The growing employment of multi-dimensional criteria of success in evaluation studies would seem to point to some fundamental changes in the grounds for action in the aims and objectives of the justice system. Indeed, there is evidence of cross fertilization taking place. Thus, risk prediction scales developed in practice are used by researchers to measure the success of programmes aimed at diverting high tariff clients from custody, whilst their further refinement in research encourages practitioners to use them for identifying clients with the highest risk (Mair 1989a).

The Interpretation of Outcomes: Practice and Context

Martinson's failure to find anything which clearly and unequivocally 'worked' is now understood to follow from one further simplification on his part, namely, his omission "to address the issue of how sentences are implemented and operate in practice" (Mair 1991b).

His thesis rested on the presumption that disposals are implemented as planned, with no consideration given to what happens in the process of implementation - the training and commitment of staff, the level of resources, the support and co-operation of other agencies. Similarly, there is a presumption that there is no variation between different agencies in the actual plans they draw up by which to implement the same disposals.

On the contrary, so Mair argues, the process of implementation may be crucial to understanding why some penal measures work well and why others fail, or why some may be seen to succeed at one time and place but, for no apparent reason, fail to succeed elsewhere. Disposals cannot be said to work or not to work, then, without consideration of the context in which they are implemented. Indeed, it may be that the context, procedures and quality of implementation bear more responsibility for the outcome than the intrinsic nature of the penal disposal.

In their review of the rehabilitation literature for 1981-7, for example, Gendreau and Ross (1987) take account of the differences between programmes in terms of the skill level of staff, the atmosphere in which they are conducted, and the clarity of their purpose, before any conclusions as to their success are drawn.

Marshall and Perry (1990) also reflect on the great difficulty in trying to evaluate mediation schemes because of the lack of any one clear statement of purpose. In their case, they do not argue that there should be only one set of objectives but rather that, as with most community based measures which have inbuilt flexibility and innovatory approaches, any evaluation has to be based on the recognition that these may compete with more traditional conceptions of criminal justice.

In her evaluative study of 12 community service schemes in Scotland, McIvor (1989) points to the largely descriptive nature of previous research on community service and its failure to demonstrate whether different approaches to the operation of community schemes are differentially effective. She redresses the situation by investigating systematic differences between community service schemes in the effectiveness of their practice to explain variations in their success rate.

In another Scottish study, Stedward and Millar (1989) recognise the contribution to the implementation of diversionary schemes of the different assumptions and ideas maintained by key personnel such as prosecutors, social workers etc. The way in which personnel worked together, the decisions made about who should be eligible for a diversionary scheme and so on were all influenced by the working philosophies of key actors.

In his five year evaluation study of the Afan alternative to custody project for 17-20 year old offenders, Raynor (1988) pays particular attention to those features in the operation of the scheme which contributed both positively and negatively to its effectiveness. Indeed, he makes them an integral part of his analysis.

Similarly, the question of resources has been a continuing issue for those concerned to realistically implement community based strategies, and research literature has a contribution to make here as well. In his study of the Children's Hearing System, Lockyer (1989) looks at how perceived deficiencies in resources, facilities and services constrain the decision making of Children's Panel members. In almost a fifth of all cases the decisions made were directly influenced by the availability of adequate resources for the implementation of the decision. Projecting this to the whole of Scotland the significance of the resource issue can be clearly understood and appreciated.

What we see in the current research literature is a reluctance to treat the measure imposed in abstraction from the context in which it is being implemented. It is likely that this reluctance will develop into a growing movement as the search for a few magic formulae subsides - a theme which will be picked up in later sections of this chapter.

Findings

The previous sections have identified some of the new approaches to research and evaluation. We now turn to recent findings and current interpretations of past findings. For analytical purposes, these findings may be divided into those which deal with:

Context;
Content; and
Clients.

As we shall see, however, the research points increasingly to the difficulty of isolating these categories from each other in practice.

(i) Context and Outcomes.

The importance of context and practice for outcome is finding an increasingly prominent position on the research agenda.

(a) Clarity and Consistency of Aims and Practice.

It seems probable that outcome is influenced in large measure by **how** effectively programmes are implemented, whatever their design or objectives.

What is crucial for the achievement of positive results, argues Gottschalk (1987) in his meta-analysis of 90 studies of community based interventions with young offenders, is that programmes are implemented as they were originally intended. His general finding may be more graphically illustrated by McIvor's finding, in her study of community service in Scotland (1989), that absences from community service depended not on the length of the order but on whether it was taking longer to complete than was originally intended. It is the adherence to an agreed plan, and not the plan itself which is decisive. For this to happen, several conditions must be met.

Firstly, objectives and measures taken to achieve them, must be clearly defined at the outset of any disposal or programme.

Secondly they must be followed consistently. Carnie (1990) shows the way in which the stated intention and aims of a measure - in his case community service - can be undermined by the views and ideas of a few key officials. In Carnie's study, community service was used in one out of five cases by sheriffs as a sentence in its own right and not as an alternative to custody.

Consistency appears to be comprised of a number of facets.

Consistency in personnel is not a sufficient condition for success but it may be a necessary one. For example, a recent study of probation in Scotland found that rapid turnover in social work departments administering probation disposals was associated with poor outcomes (Ditton 1989) - "persistent offenders require persistent social workers." Rapid turnover is also associated with poor work morale. This may provide an additional explanation for the association between personnel, consistency and outcome.

Enforcement the exercise of control to ensure that the disposal is used as intended, has important consequences for outcomes. Thus, as mentioned earlier, McIvor found that a swift response to unacceptable absences in their fulfilment of community service orders resulted in the increased compliance of clients.

Resources required to implement the programme must be available. Thus, in a related area, Lockyer found that one in five Children's Panel members felt their decisions about the need for measures of care for children were constrained by a perceived lack of resources.

(b) Interagency Co-operation.

Crucial to the success of community based disposals is the co-operation of all relevant agencies (Raynor 1988, Ditton 1989). In his study of probation in Scotland, Ditton

(1989) found that sheriffs would use probation more often if social workers made more recommendations for it and if sheriffs had greater confidence in social work supervision. Ditton also lists the ways in which confidence could be promoted and interagency links improved.

In relation to programmes on the Continent, and in particular Germany and Austria, Pelikan (1990) makes the point that there is a difference between projects which involve voluntary agencies rather than statutory agencies in implementing mediation and reparation measures. Not only are results more encouraging where voluntary agencies are involved in terms of the agreement to participate in the schemes but the results in terms of the future offending of the participants also appear to be enhanced.

Voluntary agencies are seen to have a very different way of working with clients and are also not associated with the formal authorities. The probation service in England and Wales is seen to be resistant to some community based measures because it involves working with other agencies and because the nature of the work undertaken is also seen as a threat to the professional integrity of the probation service (Whitehead et al. 1991, The Rainer Foundation 1991).

Professional and ideological conflicts are a major determining factor in the success or otherwise of measures for offenders. Whitehead et al. (1991) confirm this in their work on temporary release in the Cleveland area and The Rainer Foundation agrees that the success or otherwise of projects is determined very much by the way in which agencies, particularly statutory agencies, work both with each other and with those in the non-statutory sector. The success of its young offenders project in Aylesbury in which project workers participated with probation officers in tackling the housing and employment needs of young offenders as well as their offence behaviour, is attributed to this as is the failure of a similar project in Salford.

Raynor's findings (1988) are particularly instructive because he was able to evaluate the Afan Alternative to Custody programme over five years as well as to contrast it with an IT project in the locality, thus providing comparisons over time and between projects. He found a strong association between outcome and the strength, range and operational involvement of local contacts. The poorer outcomes achieved by the Alternative to Custody programme in its last two years are explained not by the decline in its novelty value but by the lower local involvement at that time. The significance of decentralisation in terms of allowing for local autonomy in the development of strategies and in their implementation can be illustrated in two ways.

First, particularly where voluntary organisations are involved, the lack of a hierarchical line management structure allows programmes to be formulated in response to local factors and also to be implemented by deploying local resources. The flexibility of operation of voluntary organisations is seen to be a considerable asset.

Secondly, locating programmes firmly in the community allows for working relationships to evolve across professional and other boundaries. In the light of the drive in the late 1980's for a more community based approach, we cannot highlight strongly enough the significance of local resources and factors in influencing the success of a project.

For any project to make an impact on sentencing, Raynor (1988) demonstrates how important it is that sentencers, social workers and probation officers see it as a viable and constructive option. This requires the promotion and reinforcement of interagency links by project staff to ensure an adequate input of appropriate cases. It also requires that encouragement not only be given to use them but that discouragement be made from using other options which the alternatives are intended to replace. Thus, Raynor found that unlike the Afan young adult offenders programme, the objectives of the local IT project were not met. This was not because of some deficiency in the programme itself but because its objectives had not been built into other important parts of the juvenile justice system.

Similarly, Curtis (1992) argues that the reason that we fail to use non custodial alternatives as often as we should is that custody is resourced and financed in such a way as to make it difficult for sentencers to conceive of using other measures.

The implications of all this for an understanding of the association between context and outcome are:

> no part of the criminal justice system can be treated in isolation;

> good interagency links are more likely if programmes operate at the local level so that they are co-terminous with as few court, probation or social work teams as possible. The less diffuse the interagency links, the more it is likely that sensitive and responsive relationships will be promoted and maintained over time.

(c) The Attributes of Staff, the Quality of Practice and Social Organisation.

The attributes of staff have also been found to influence outcomes. Sinclair (1991) for example, found the personal qualities of probation hostel wardens to be the major determinant of the effectiveness of a hostel. This has two implications.

First, it is useful to know the attributes of individuals which are associated with positive outcomes. In probation hostels Sinclair (1991) found it to be wardens who combined kindness with strict discipline; in an intensive probation programme for young adults, Raynor (1988) found it to be commitment combined with energy; and in the Scottish context, Ditton (1989) found it to be social workers whose interest in probation and working with offenders was paramount. Though **personal** attributes are being treated as significant, the implication of these findings nevertheless point to the way in which context can be influenced through the careful selection and training of staff.

Second, attributes of staff allow researchers to investigate the ways in which different social organizations promote or discourage personal attributes and qualities of practice desirable for the realisation of different penal objectives.

Again, referring to the findings of European researchers such as Pelikan (1990), voluntary organisations can play a role in the development of community based measures of a different nature from that of the statutory agencies. The Rainer Foundation confirms that a key feature of their programmes is the personal commitment, skills and expertise of their workers. The National Children's Home in Scotland also identifies the need to provide good quality social work by appointing the right people to manage and run projects.

On the basis of the research available, the contracting out to voluntary agencies of much of the responsibility for dealing with offenders may well have the additional benefit of improved service provision as a result of careful selection and training of project workers. Carnie (1990) illustrates clearly the dismay expressed by sheriffs at the unacceptable delays in the handling of cases and that the use of community service depends as much on the credibility of the programme as anything else. To this end, sheriffs themselves had expressed the wish to find out more about actual projects and to be involved with project workers. (This is a feature of the project that was built in from the beginning by the NCH with their Dundee project).

(ii) Content and Outcome.

(a) Diversion

Richardson and Tutt (1991) repeating what many commentators have asserted, comment that:

"there can be no doubt.... that the message from the last decade is that the policy of diversion from court has been a major success" (p7).

Nevertheless, a number of questions have to be asked of the way in which diversion operates and on whom diversionary strategies are targeted.

A thorough literature review of sanction effectiveness for persistent and serious offenders was completed recently by McIvor (1990). The central criterion employed by McIvor in her treatment of sanctions for young offenders is recidivism, and this is probably accurate in reflecting the focus of the literature reviewed. However, she does give consideration in her review to the other objectives of penal measures, especially as they aim to divert young people from criminal justice processing or from institutionalisation. She cites many examples of 'net widening' and 'creaming off' and most properly concludes with a warning that in the implementation of these sanctions:

"Care should be taken to ensure that programmes that are designed to divert young offenders from various points in the criminal justice system are appropriately targeted to achieve these goals" (p36).

It is instructive to explore the literature further, however, to identify common characteristics amongst those programmes which report success in achieving their diversionary objectives. The Afan Alternative, for example, reported a substantial reduction of 40% in custodial outcomes in the local Afan Magistrates Court over a five year period - a reduction which was not replicated in the rest of West Glamorgan (Raynor 1988). The two 1987 census surveys of schemes for juvenile offenders (England and Wales) funded under the DHSS IT Initiative, found the custody rates for males (14-16) in initiative areas to be 9.3% of those found guilty of an indictable offence, compared with 11.4% nationally (NACRO,1989). Thus, both the Afan Alternative and the IT Initiative provided sentencers not just with an additional disposal -an alternative to custody - but was actually seen to be replacing custody as a disposal.

Nor was net widening in evidence - the tariff position of Afan project recruits was reported to resemble more closely young adult offenders sentenced to custody than to community service or 'normal' probation. The number and type of previous disposals received by those attending IT projects in 1987, and the types of offences they committed, show them to be similar for those receiving custody and care - except for crimes of violence which is under-represented. Indeed, the proportion of males attending projects with three or more disposals was seen to have risen by over 12% over the year, "confirmation that the projects are increasingly working with the persistent offenders they were set up to manage".

Reduction of custody and prevention of net widening depend, firstly, upon successful interagency recruitment - sentencers must be willing to replace custody with non-custodial sanctions for those previously receiving custody. The strategies adopted to achieve this will largely depend on the local context.

In Afan, for example, a disciplined framework, a demanding context and strict expectations of attendance were all thought to be necessary to ensure the co-operation and participation of magistrates. This points to the importance of contextual factors for outcome over and above that which was already set out above, particularly, interagency co-operation. The substance of the programme itself must be oriented to and constructed around the recruitment and support of other players and other arenas within the criminal justice system.

Secondly, successful diversion requires that target clientele be correctly identified and off-target referrals rejected. Day centres in England and Wales, for example, were found to vary widely (Mair 1989) in diverting young offenders from custody and resisting net widening. Successful day centres were those accepting very specific target groups identified by using statistically validated risk of custody scales.

In relation to the review of mediation and reparation schemes, Marshall and Perry (1990) show that high participation rates of offender and victim can often be attributed not to the appeal of the programme but because very little is expected of both parties. For example, differentiating between *police based* and *court based* approaches to mediation, they argue that high participation rates in police programmes can be attributed to the fact such programmes generally adopt an approach to mediation that involves little more than a formal apology and a handshake. The more demanding (but seen also to be more rewarding court based approaches) inevitably appeal to a possibly smaller and potentially very different section of the community.

In sum, successful diversion from criminal processing or institutionalisation requires that both interagency co-operation and accurate targeting methods be built into the implementation and content of diversionary measures.

(b) Recidivism

A few general principles may be drawn from research literature regarding the effectiveness of differing measures in reducing recidivism amongst young offenders.

In her extensive review of the literature, McIvor (1990) found little evidence to support deterrent approaches amongst younger age groups. Punitive institutional regimes appear to have had little impact on re-offending amongst younger age groups while shock probation or "scared straight" programmes give no cause for encouragement.

Monetary sanctions (restitution) and community service appear to be at least as effective as probation and custody in reducing offending (McIvor 1990).

Community integration is identified as an important component of those penal measures which are effective in reducing re-offending in the younger age groups. The Hereford and Worcester intensive probation programme (Roberts 1989), established for young unemployed offenders at high risk of custody, may be cited as a case in point. Offenders were obliged to attend the programme three days a week with a fourth day devoted to involvement in projects aimed at establishing links and enhancing integration into the local community. Compared with a control group, these intensive probationers were less often and less quickly involved in criminal behaviour. In sum, the more the community is actually built into community based disposals, the more likely they are to be successful on the recidivist criterion. Community based measures require to be in the community more than by name alone.

Amongst younger age groups, family interventions and other attempts to work with them in their social networks have met with some success.

Amongst older offenders, peer group approaches based on a problem solving model, offence-focused, involving high quality but authoritative relationships, and concerned with the development of personal and social skills are associated with reduced offending. By contrast, those based on a deterrence model, where good but non-authoritative relationships are achieved and where counselling is non-directive have negligible effects.

From amongst those factors associated with success, Gordon and Arbuthnott (1987) focus in their review upon the problem behaviour of individual, group and family interventions with juvenile offenders. They suggest that even modest success in community based disposals depends upon an ecological assessment of the problem behaviour, setting up behavioural goals related to the problem for which the offender is referred, structured teaching of skills directly related to the problem behaviour and the practice of these skills in the problem setting.

(iii)   Client Groups and Outcome.

Claims made for the effectiveness of different disposals for young offenders are promising but they are tempered by a growing recognition that the client group is by no means homogeneous. Indeed, we may now be seeing a move to a position of searching for what specifically works for different categories of young offenders.

This approach arises directly out of the research literature which indicates that offenders,

"who have different needs or are differentially involved in offending behaviour respond differently to different sanctions or approaches" (McIvor, 1990).

Thus, Baskwell (1976, 1980) found recidivism rates to be higher amongst young offenders where treatment was not matched to the client than amongst offenders who received only minimal treatment with surveillance. Intervention with no respect for the diversity of the client group, then, is the worst of all possible worlds.

Intensive programmes are now believed to benefit older, more experienced high risk young offenders while at the same time having negative effects on low risk cases. The findings of a series of research projects on intensive probation (including Roberts (1989) and Raynor (1988) in England and Wales) show that it is best reserved for higher risk cases. Lower risk young offenders may actually be harmed, both by the restrictiveness and labelling consequences of the programme, and by their exposure to offenders more deeply involved in delinquent behaviour.

That intensive group work is more effective with higher risk offenders is consistent with the 'risk principle' of supervision emerging from the studies of Andrews et al. (1986) in Ontario - the higher the risk of recidivism, the more appropriate and effective are intensive measures. The application of the risk principle to practice has required that risk assessment instruments be developed so as to identify young offenders with high risk of offending just as they have been done to identify those with high risk of custody.

Young offenders also respond differently according to their problems and needs. The British IMPACT study (Folkard et al. 1974) examined the effects on recidivism of randomly allocating probationers to programmes of varying intensity. The intensive programme was most successful in reducing recidivism amongst those who regarded themselves as having many problems, but were also rated as having low criminal tendencies. Normal supervision conditions were most effective with probationers who regarded themselves as having few problems but had high criminal tendencies. When needs are taken into consideration, then, young offenders with low risk of recidivism did better in intensive programmes and those with high risk of recidivism did better under normal supervision. To achieve the best outcome, therefore, both risk and need should be taken into consideration prior to allocation.

More recent research on enhanced probation has also shown the potential for probation programmes to reduce the custodial rate and to increase the number of cases diverted (Creamer, Hartley and McWilliams 1992).

If young offenders respond variously to different programmes according to their needs or their involvement in offending behaviour, the research suggests that sanctions and approaches must be established which orient to a wide variety of needs and to all levels of delinquency.

The research undertaken by Coates et al. (1978, 1981), for example, locates lower recidivism rates in those areas which had developed greater diversity of community based options for young offenders than those areas in which resources were concentrated in one or two different types of programme. A strong feeling is emerging in the literature, however, that true diversity cannot be established without clarification of the differences between measures and programmes.

IT projects for example, need to establish whether they are dealing with troubled or troublesome children, (Bennett-Emslie et al. 1990) and Senior Attendance Centres and Day Centres should more clearly orient their programmes so that they serve different client groups. In sum, diversity is only successful in so far as a clear division of labour vis a vis different client groups is established (Mair 1989b). NACRO goes further than this in stating that the effect on reoffending rates could be noticeable where projects are governed by single, simple or clear statements of purpose (1990).

With specific reference to the unemployed offender, bearing in mind the fact that many young adult offenders are likely to be unemployed, there is a growing body of evidence pointing to the fact that the unemployed are ordered to do more hours of community service than others (Jardine 1983; Moxon 1988). The concern about this expressed by NACRO (1989) and others (Hoggarth 1991) is twofold.

First, that the community service order may well be being used for the unemployed mainly because it is viewed as providing useful work experience and training.

Second, that because of this and for other reasons, the community service order may be being used not as an alternative to custody but as an alternative to other sentences.

Summary

In this chapter, we have identified a number of themes common to the literature and which we believe should be taken into consideration in any attempt to identify or devise measures for young adult offenders.

1 Factors other than recidivism are significant in the evaluation of community based measures.

2 Measures do not operate in a vacuum. Their success or failure may depend as much on the context in which they operate, as on the measures themselves.

3 Without interagency co-operation the success of specific measures will be seriously inhibited because of the difficulty of: working across professional boundaries; professional and ideological conflicts; the lack of knowledge held by certain groupings about the work and activities of others; the ignorance about just what measures are available in the community and how they operate.

4 The voluntary sector has an important role to play in the development and implementation of community based measures because it is not associated with the formal statutory authorities and, for that reason, it can operate in a more flexible and responsive manner.

5 Projects and measures with a decidedly local orientation, deploying local resources, will be more likely to be successful.

6 The quality of personnel and service provision is an important variable determining the success or otherwise of measures.

7 Measures operate better with clear, simple objectives and aims.

Chapter Three

Reductionist Strategies

The Growth of Diversion

There can be little doubt about the growth of diversionary strategies over the past twenty years. Most European countries have developed measures both to divert offenders from the criminal justice system and to reduce the numbers of offenders entering custody.

The significance of diversionary strategies has been well documented by a number of commentators (Feest 1990, Richardson and Tutt 1991, Pratt 1983, 1986) as have been the shifts in legal and penal thinking which have accompanied them. Pelikan (1990) for example documents the way in which the growth in diversionary strategies has meant a shift from the **principle of legality** to the **principle of discretion**.

The implication of this is that whereas there are seen to be undoubted benefits from the development of diversion, there is also considerable concern that this may mean that the rights of individual offenders are being given insufficient protection. As more and more measures, as Bailleau and Garioud (1990) had anticipated, are implemented outwith the criminal justice system, offenders may not be given the protection of due process of law available to others.

Smith and Gill (1989) also comment that the search for community based alternatives and the general move to diversion has been generally accompanied by a lack of adequate resources either to expand the network of existing services or to develop innovative programmes.

In this review we intend to use a modified version of Feest's (1990) classification scheme referred to above. Feest's scheme is useful in allowing us to list the types of diversionary measures available and to present examples. However, it has the major drawback that crime prevention and social crime prevention programmes get insufficient coverage.

In many respects, his first classification of **entry avoidance** could be taken to refer to those social crime prevention programmes which have as one of their objectives the amelioration of the social and economic conditions in which young people most at risk find themselves. these are given fuller discussion in the next section.

In considering the types of measures available, a number of questions have to be borne in mind. In particular, diversionary measures have to analysed in terms of their target population; what is the focus of attention - the offence or the individual; how far can it achieve its stated objectives?

Diversionary Measures

Diversion can take a number of forms. It can refer for example to:

diversion from the criminal justice system as such and does not involve any decision on the part of personnel within it;

diversion from the criminal justice system which is in some way dependent on the agreement of key personnel such as the police or the prosecution service; and

diversion at the point of sentencing or from custody (the two are not necessarily the same).

In what follows, examples of the three forms will be illustrated. It has to be said though that how the measures referred to should be categorised may be debatable given the form that some of them take.

(i) Entry Avoidance.

The Stewart Committee (1983) recommended the use of a fixed penalty system and the use of warnings, both formal and informal, from the police and by the procurator fiscal, and these would fit neatly into Feest's classificatory schema. What can also be included here is the extended use of the police caution, a measure employed more in England and Wales than in any other European country. Moreover, the growth in use of the police caution has also been seen as one of the characteristics of the development of diversionary measures.

Feest would also include the use of privatised justice (see also Bailleau and Garioud 1990) in which private organisations discipline their own members or in which the behaviour of customers (e.g.. fare-dodgers) could be regulated. It could also be taken to refer to a greater degree of toleration shown to certain behaviours such as the taking of drugs or alcohol abuse and to the decision to waive prosecution completely (Joutsen 1991).

(ii) Process Interruption.

Process interruption refers to those measures which depend on the participation of personnel in the criminal justice system to allow cases to be dealt with elsewhere and can take a variety of forms (Feest 1990). Examples include those strategies which involve the young offender participating in community based alternatives before becoming fully implicated in the criminal justice process. Mediation, reparation and reconciliation, however, are the most prevalent of such schemes and, though they may also fall under the classification of conviction and sentencing avoidance, reference will be made to some examples in this section.

(a) Extra Judicial Processes.

In referring to diversion from prosecution, Stedward and Millar (1989) have described the availability of social work diversion schemes in Scotland as dependent on negotiation between the procurators fiscal and the social work department. In this programme, offenders could be diverted to social work departments for counselling or case work. One of the key elements from the description of the schemes given by Stedward and Millar is that fairly minor cases were involved with shoplifting, breach of the peace, drunk and incapable and assault constituting most of the cases.

Moreover, very few men between the age of 16 and 30 were diverted under these schemes which appeared to be used more for women and the older offender with few previous convictions. It does seem to be a characteristic of diversionary schemes and community based disposals where these are different, that young offenders between the ages of 16 and 25 are excluded more often than not from participation. More recent information though suggests that almost 16% of those diverted to social work in Edinburgh were between 16 and 21, with almost 35% being between 21 and 30 - a slightly different profile.

In relation to other measures such as community service, young offenders are seldom given the opportunity to participate (Hoggarth 1991). It is interesting to speculate as to why this might be the case - whether there is a set of assumptions and ideologies about crime by young people which does not readily accommodate them within measures and programmes outwith the criminal justice arena. It may well be that it is the same line of thinking which sees few young offenders of 16 and 17 remaining within the Children's Hearings system in Scotland when there is legislative backing for them to do so.

As Stedward and Millar point out, diversion was seen to be more of a welfare oriented measure and one in which, because there was no time delay with cases going to court, the offence was fresh in the mind of the offender with whom task centred, intensive work could be carried out. The benefits were seen by procurators fiscal and others to be a reduction in recidivism as well as the provision of assistance and a reduction of the cost to the criminal justice system.

The danger with many of these forms of programmes, as the research literature had shown, is that of **net widening.** In the case of the Scottish diversion schemes what is implied is that, because the scheme is meant to operate on the needs of the offender, some offenders may be included who might **not** otherwise have been the subject of prosecution. Joutsen (1991) identifies the waiving of prosecution completely when it is not in the interests of the state to prosecute or when the negative aspects of prosecution would far outweigh the gains, as an important contribution in the Danish criminal justice system to reducing the number of people going, unnecessarily he would say, through the system.

The Halt programme against vandalism in the Netherlands was first introduced in Rotterdam in 1981 and was designed to allow offenders the opportunity of either entering the programme or proceeding through the more traditional form of criminal (and perhaps judicial) proceedings. Under the Halt banner, offenders between the age of 12 and 18 can be:

"given the option of avoiding traditional criminal proceedings providing they participate in alternate activities and make good the damage done, at least in part" (Ministrie de Justitie 1989, p2).

Where the offender fails to complete the programme, the prosecutor retains the right to pursue the case through the traditional channels as is the case in the diversion schemes in Scotland discussed above.

The success and just as importantly, the acceptability of the Halt programme is illustrated by the fact that by 1989, 45 Halt programmes had been established in municipalities in the Netherlands with a total of over seven million inhabitants. Funding is secured from the Ministry of Justice and the municipality with the offender contributing indirectly by reducing the costs of clearing up any damage or vandalism. The offender is involved in clearing up directly any damage done but is also seen to be paying back something to the community through involvement in the scheme.

Moreover, the Dutch have also included the Halt scheme in their preventive strategies. When an offender enters the Halt programme details are taken of the situation and the personal and social circumstances of the offence and an attempt made to ameliorate these to reduce the possibility of repetition.

The acceptability of the scheme is aided by the knowledge that almost 42% of those in the scheme subsequently commit fewer acts of vandalism and 20% stop altogether. For these reasons it is seen to meet the criteria of reducing the volume of cases going through the system but also directly contributes to a reduction in offence behaviour.

Though slightly different in orientation, Denmark (**Vestergard forthcoming**) has also introduced a system of **juvenile contracts** for young offenders who have not yet entered fully on a criminal career. The offender undertakes to do some work which must be "immediately perceptible and relevant". Examples include participation in municipal employment projects, employment with the railway system, working for a private employer, etc.

The details of the contract are drawn up between the offender, his family and the social authorities. The obvious "carrot" is that successful completion of the contract means that there is no stigma of a criminal record. It also highlights one of the features of many diversionary measures and of community based measures themselves

- that is, the significance of the ideology of work and the benefits to be achieved in gainful employment. This is perhaps what Faugeron and Houchon (1987) mean by "the utopia of regenerative toil".

(b) Mediation and Reparation.

The growth of diversionary measures has been particularly marked in mediation and reparation with most European countries having introduced some form of programme in recent years (see Marshall and Perry 1990, Walgrave et al.; Joutsen 1991; Pelikan 1989; Warner 1992). Mediation is taken to refer to the practice of third parties helping two or more parties resolve a conflict. Reparation refers to some form of paying back either in kind or in some material way. The history of the development of mediation and reparation shows that they have often gone hand in hand with the conflict between offender and victim being resolved through some form of mediation (Marshall and Merry 1990). Marshall and Walpole (1985) give a useful review of the development of mediation schemes in the UK.

Moreover, some criminal justice systems are contemplating the creation of multifaceted measures based on a mixture of elements of different measures. The Dutch for example, are considering the possibility of measures which would consist of community service, a skill training programme, the obligation to pay restitution, mediation and probation and so on. (Alternative sanctions to decrease prison overcrowding in Holland, 1991).

For the most part, mediation measures are offered at the point where prosecution is being considered, though the judiciary may also opt for mediation and reparation. Marshall and Merry (1990) for example differentiate between those schemes which involve diversion from prosecution to mediation schemes at the point of prosecution or at sentence. Warner (1992) reports on a scheme to divert minor cases from prosecution by referring them to the SACRO reparation and mediation project. Amongst the conclusions drawn were that in a study of the comparative costs of reparation and mediation and court, the SACRO project was not a cheap alternative to prosecution. The evaluation however showed that reparation and mediation is an acceptable and effective response to minor crime and can be used to divert certain minor cases. Victims, accused and fiscals were all satisfied with the process and outcome and, what must surely be a prime consideration, also felt that justice had been done.

In relation to diversion from custody for more serious cases, the work of Creamer, Hartley and McWilliams (1992) in evaluating an enhanced probation scheme clearly shows the benfits in creating an "alternative to custody ethos" whereby "social workers and courts are increasingly prepared to consider a range of community disposals in the more serious cases as diversions from custody" (p 95).

Pelikan (1989) claims that the development of measures such as mediation took place at a time when the number of cases in which prosecution was waived was, in any case, going down. Prosecutors had been encouraged (see Joutsen 1991) to waive prosecution at a time when the numbers of minor offences were going up and were presenting the problem of potential overload for the criminal justice system. The use of measures such as mediation, though, have to be seen in terms of a very different perception and handling of cases.

The development of mediation and related measures have to be seen in the light of the acceptance generally of non judicial forms of dispute resolution such as the growth of mediation and reconciliation for other social groups including those divorced or separated and those in dispute over the custody of children. In that respect, mediation schemes have introduced a conception of justice that is less coercive and power laden than traditional criminal justice and is more concerned to promote dialogue and equity in the resolution of conflicts (De Cauter 1991).

Such measures also have to be seen with reference to the work of Nils Christie who argues that the state has "appropriated conflicts" and that informal dispute resolution "gives back" to the individual responsibility for determining what happens in the event of conflict. The re-appropriation of conflicts involves the injured party in expressing the nature of compensation wanted from the person who caused the damage or hurt. Before giving examples of the variety of forms that mediation may take, it is perhaps worth identifying the key principles on which most mediation and related measures are based.

In most mediation schemes, offenders are assumed to be responsible for what they have done and this is taken into account in also allowing them to be involved in negotiation over just what should happen. This is also reflected in the fact that participation in schemes is usually voluntary.

The victim is also involved in the negotiations where appropriate, though as we shall see this involvement can take a variety of forms. Many schemes are in fact based on concern that the victim's needs and wishes are taken into consideration. For example, the SOS Aggressions Conflits in Paris (Marshall and Merry 1990) operates with the victim very much in mind and the Strasbourg ACCORD scheme operates entirely outwith the criminal justice system and allows for mediation to be requested by either the victim or the offender.

In Scotland there are very few mediation/reparation schemes. More information on the variety and forms such schemes take can be found in the plethora of such arrangements in England and Wales and in the rest of Europe. Mackay (1986, 1988) and Warner (1992) do, however, provide useful information on the pilot scheme organised by SACRO in the Lothian and Strathclyde region. The Lothian scheme allows for offenders and victims to be offered the opportunity of referral to a mediation scheme at the point where a decision to prosecute is being made. Most of the schemes south of the border are either police or court based and few are like the SACRO scheme in being pre-trial.

Marshall and Merry (1990) point to the fact that in the UK, referral to mediation or reparation schemes can take a variety of forms and can include:

those offenders who are involved in schemes before they get into the criminal justice system proper (such as mediation schemes for those referred from police juvenile liaison);

picking up cases before a court hearing from amongst offenders who admit their guilt (such as the Totten scheme in Hampshire). This allows for cases to be dealt with within a much shorter time scale from the committal of the offence;

offenders being referred as a sentence of the court (as in the case of the Rochdale and Bury scheme in Greater Manchester). In addition, as they too indicate (though it cannot be called a combined order) there are those young people who are referred to Intermediate Treatment schemes by the court:

"who show signs of incipient criminal careers and who are in danger of incarceration, and which employ varied packages of intensive social work, counselling, educational and other techniques, may on occasion use a meeting with the victim, if this can be arranged, in order to impress on the offender the real harm done" (p12/13).

An example of such a strategy is the Woodlands Centre scheme in Hampshire.

In their review of projects in England Wales, many of which are funded by the Home Office, Marshall and Merry (1990) further classify mediation and reparation projects into police based and court based.

The police based schemes such as the Exeter Youth Support Project, the Cumbria Reparation Scheme and the Sandiwell Urban Programme all have in common the fact that they take offenders who have been referred from police juvenile liaison schemes. They also operate on the basis of integration and co-operation between the police, local authority social services and the probation service and generally have the objective of diverting the offender from prosecution and ultimately from the potential of custody. Diversion from prosecution is the main objective and offenders are as far as possible to be helped to re-integrate into the community; mediation is one part of this process.

Court based schemes are those which involve the court in deciding whether or not the offender should be referred to a mediation scheme. The Coventry Reparation Scheme, the Leeds Reparation Project and the Wolverhampton Reparation Project, all reviewed by Marshall and Merry, are examples of the court based approach. In these schemes, the offender can be referred to a mediation scheme whilst the court awaits the completion of a Social Inquiry Report and during the three week period involved successful completion of the mediation process will mean that this is taken into consideration in sentencing. The much closer relationship between the offence and the mediation process is seen to be a distinct advantage over more traditional approaches which could well involve the offender in a protracted process. (See Carnie 1990 on the views of sheriffs in this respect).

A crucial variable is that in most forms of mediation, the process is directed by personnel not associated with the court, usually from voluntary organisations and sometimes volunteers. The exception are those police based mediation programmes. (See for example the Exeter Joint Services Support Team in Marshall and Perry, op cit., p41) which may well be the responsibility of individual police officers. Again, as we shall see, the nature of the supervising agency and its relationship to the formal authorities can have an influence on the success or otherwise of the operation of the scheme.

(c) European Schemes.

The reduction of the prison population in what was West Germany can be put down in part to the expansion of diversionary alternatives amongst which were a variety of mediation type programmes. The Brucke package of measures in Munich (Pelikan 1989) offered three types of mediation programmes and these were:

Victim oriented;
Offender oriented; and
conflict resolution schemes.

One of the key features of the Brucke and other mediation schemes is that they were financed by independent welfare organisations. The significance of this is best appreciated by comparing the efforts of the Cologne Waage-Projekt and the Braunschweig (Pelikan 1989).

In the Cologne project, mediation schemes involved diversionary decisions by prosecutors and judges to projects which were set up, devised and run by the equivalent of the British voluntary agencies. The project was seen to have a high participation rate (90-95% victim and offender participation rate) and reparation agreed between victims and offenders involved other than cash transfers. In relation to the high participation rate, Dunkel (1991) notes that there is a general acceptance of the merit of mediation and reparation programmes and that victims are very keen to be involved. Such a claim is repeated by Fischer & Jeune (1987) in their evaluation of a Canadian victim offender project and by Warner in the Scottish context.

The success of the Cologne project meant that there are now similar schemes operating for adult offenders, but it has to be remembered that in terms of German criminal law, these schemes which were to apply to juveniles include those up to 20 who would be considered in the UK to be young adults.

The Braunschweig scheme, with diversion only from prosecution, referred to by Pelikan was, in contrast, a failure with the possibility of funding being withdrawn. The main reason postulated for the failure is the close association of the criminal justice system with the project, and the failure to achieve the level of impartiality apparent in the Cologne project which had the involvement of voluntary agencies. Dunkel (1990) also suggests that projects be differentiated by whether they are offered by private organisations or by more official representatives of the state because of the significance this has for their success.

What these two projects have in common with others in West Germany such as the Reutlingen Project Handschlag (Project Handshake) is that offenders have to perform some form of reparation, do some form of community service, make financial reparation, and that the reparation has a symbolic as much as a material significance.

Pelikan (1989) also draws our attention, in comparing the West German schemes with the evolution of mediation in Austria, to the fact that out of court resolution of conflicts does indeed involve a very different way of conceiving of how cases are handled. For example, unlike the traditional course taken in social work and probation, mediation does not entail "looking at and digging up the past". The process requires offenders to accept responsibility for what they have done (indeed the Braunschweig project only accepts offenders who have unsollicitedly confessed their crime).

Also, she argues that mediation processes will work far better if they are separated from other measures or orders and that it is the process of mediation that brings about changes in the offender. Confronting the situation requires the offender to operate in the real world and not removed from it by resort to ultra theoretical explanations about behaviour. McIvor's (1990) work on the community service order in Scotland suggests something similar. Moreover and perhaps more importantly, work has to be undertaken with both offender and victim in such a way that:

> *"activates and restores the capacities of the parties involved to negotiate this conflict and any future conflicts without further assistance from the state and the helping professions."* (Pelikan 1989).

Similar thinking underpins the expansion of mediation in Finland (Joutsen 1991) and most other European countries and they reflect Joutsen's commitment that the Finnish approach will continue to move away from a legalistic and rigid system to one where the principle of minimum intervention prevails.

Unlike most of the German and Austrian schemes, Belgium has a number of schemes through which offenders are referred **by the judiciary** to a mediation programme. Though this operates in the jurisdiction of the juvenile court, we have to bear in mind once again that this refers to young people up to 18. The main point to make here is that a decision to refer to the Arpege conciliation scheme is a matter for the juvenile court to decide, and not as is often the case, a matter for the prosecutor (Dongier and Doosselaere 1991).

In terms of who is diverted to a mediation programme, most authorities acknowledge that it is usually offenders with few previous convictions, who have committed less serious offences and most do not accept cases that involve violent or persistent anti-social behaviours. Less a form of mediation and more a form of restitution is the Oikoten project

(Walgrave et al. 1991) the only one of its kind in Belgium. In the Oikoten scheme, the prosecutor can decide that where appropriate, offenders can be required to pay for what they have done through some form of financial compensation to the victim. Again, those referred to this scheme will have no significant criminal record and will have committed a minor offence. The benefit of restitution is that criminal proceedings are of course dropped.

In many types of mediation or reparation, offenders can and indeed do meet directly with the victims of their crime where appropriate. There are of course, many variations and in one scheme in Droitwich, known as the Individual Reparation/ Mediation video scheme a novel approach is taken to confrontation between offender and victim. Young offenders can explain their behaviour, their reasons for offending and offer an apology all on video. Victims likewise are invited to record their feelings and the video is then used to confront the offender with the reactions of the victim.

Video is also used as part of the Arpege project referred to above. Using the Montreal Metropolitan Centre Social Services Project as a model, the Arpege team (which is composed of psychologists) produced a video as an educational tool for the project with the objectives of:

> stimulating or re-stimulating adolescents' awareness that someone is a victim of their offence;

> creating the desire to meet the victim with a view to setting up a conciliation procedure whenever it is possible; and

> causing a compensatory measure to be set up in relation with the victims problems or, if the victim-offender contact is not possible, getting the offender to contact the victim.

After the viewing of the video, there is a group discussion which is used to reinforce the reality of the offending behaviour through the pressure of the group. If change in behaviour or attitude is desired then, according to the Arpege team, this is more easily achieved with the group rather than the individual.

Mediation schemes have expanded considerably on the continent in both form and content. There does however appear to be some reluctance to develop such schemes in Scotland and a number of reasons have been put forward for this. In particular, the apparent reluctance shown by prosecutors to divert offenders may be attributed to the lack of sufficiently developed alternatives. This repeats the point made above that where alternatives to prosecution, or even custody, are scarce there is a self-fulfilling prophecy that traditional forms of proceedings will continue to be used. There is in a sense, an inbuilt incentive not to seek alternatives.

(iii) Remand Avoidance.

In relation to the young adult offender, reducing the numbers sent to prison on remand would ease substantially the pressure on the prison system as well as potentially contributing to a reduction in the reoffending and reconviction rates of this group.

Examples of remand avoidance schemes are the Southend BOSS project run by the Rainer Foundation and The Blackshaw Road Project run by the London Philanthropic Society and the Borough of Wandsworth .

The BOSS (Bail Out Support Scheme) project is a joint venture involving Essex Social Services Committee and managed by the Rainer Foundation. Testimony to the apparent success of its scheme is renewal of funding for five years. The scheme is intended to provide courts with alternatives to remanding young people into custody or care where conventional bail conditions have failed. Keeping the young offender within his own community and minimising disruption of links with family or with school or the labour market are treated as main objectives. Family problems, school or work difficulties are all tackled by the BOSS workers.

The project offers close supervision and control during periods of bail and ensures that the young person attends court. When the young person is convicted, the intervention of the BOSS project means there is more chance that a non-custodial measure will be imposed.

In evaluating the scheme, Hickey and Douglas (1988) found that the scheme had a unit cost of £55.00 per week in comparison with £300.00 for a children's home, £400.00 for prison and £1000.00 for a secure unit. They also point to the way in which the scheme could only operate successfully through interagency co-operation and that an important element in the project was the contact made by members of the Foundation and of the Project with key personnel such as magistrates, social services, probation officers and solicitors.

The Blackshaw Road Project (Mason 1991) deals with more than 35 teenagers every year with a good success rate in that only half of those who have received bail support have reoffended with most offences being less serious than the original. To repeat the point that has been made throughout this review, links between the different agencies involved are identified as crucial in both the operation of the project and in the general change in thinking about how to deal with young offenders in the area served by the bench. Mason writes:

> "..and on top of receiving a significant boost in the number of people remanded on bail with their families rather than into custody, carefully nurtured links between the scheme and court officials have actually managed to change attitudes" (p vi) and;

> "One of our biggest achievements is that we have managed to establish a rapport with magistrates. They're now more prepared to put people on bail in the knowledge that we're there to help them" (p. vi).

Like the Boss project, the Blackshaw Road scheme privileges the community as the location which is most likely to reduce offending and the scheme gives young people the support to survive what the project sees as essentially a growing up phase.

Stone (1988) has been more cautious in his evaluation of remand information projects as operated by the probation service and sees them only contributing indirectly to a reduction in the use of custody. Feest (1990) also notes that remand avoidance may mean that the project involved:

"provides accommodation, work and social contacts for such people, thereby creating the legal basis for their not being remanded to prison or to be released from remand prison".

A recent Scottish initiative, again a collaborative exercise between Lothian Region and SACRO, is the BAIL INFORMATION Scheme with similar objectives to those already referred to above. An evaluation is also being carried out as the scheme proceeds.

As with the projects in the UK, remand schemes in Germany are also run by voluntary agencies and as the Rainer experience shows, the informality of the voluntary agencies and their detachment from the official and formal processes of social control does appear to be particularly advantageous.

(iv) Conviction/Sentencing Avoidance.

As Feest points out (1990, p9), when cases get to court, the theoretical possibilities for diversion are very little different from before except that the judiciary may well be involved in some way. In relation to conviction avoidance, the examples he cites include those which involve the recommendation of informal settlements, for example, the practice adopted in Greece whereby the court can halt proceedings to allow for informal settlement to be reached (p10).

Pelikan (1989) also points to the fact that the judiciary can, before proceeding with a trial, ask that cases be referred to a mediation or reparation scheme. Successful resolution through the mediation process means no further proceedings and no record of conviction. A number of commentators, including Feest have expressed concern that this approach to dealing with offenders, particularly at the court stage, will rarely be used for offenders who come before the court from lower socio-economic positions, from which most young adult offenders come. There is then the danger that a very useful means of reducing appearances in courts could be subject to the criticism of class bias in its operation. Certainly, Hoggarth (1991) and Whitehead (1991) in other contexts have made similar comments.

In relation to sentence avoidance, the best example which relates specifically to young offenders is that of the Coventry reparation scheme whereby offenders may be required (see above)to attend the scheme during the period in which a Social Enquiry Report is being prepared. Offenders, on the completion of the mediation process, may either be the subject of no further action by the court or at the very least have their sentence reduced with the possibility of avoiding custody. In that respect, the BOSS scheme and the Blackshaw Road scheme would also fit into this category because of the way in which they can assist in reducing the potential for custodial sentencing.

(v) Imprisonment Avoidance.

It is with reference to the measures designed specifically as an alternative to custody that perhaps most progress has been made in providing a variety of options for sentencers and others.

What is apparent from all the literature and from our various discussions is that very few countries in Europe, with the exception of England and Wales and the Netherlands are contemplating the use of electronic monitoring. Most of the Council of Europe countries have rejected electronic monitoring because of the anxiety that it infringes offenders rights and because electronic monitoring has a number of costs in the way in which the offender can be integrated fully and socially into the community.

(a) Sentence Reduction.

Before considering options available to sentencers it is perhaps worth pointing out that there are also schemes or practices in the UK and Europe which involve either the avoidance of custody altogether or at least early or temporary release. In relation to the former, Feest helps by identifying, through the work of Rutherford (1984), the practice of putting offenders on a waiting list for prison with the possibility of being pardoned. A further example given is of the Belgian practice whereby offenders sentenced up to a period of four months can have the application of their sentence waived at the discretion of the court.

Whitehead et al.(1991) have also completed an examination of what they have referred to as the "market leader" of the Temporary Release Scheme operated through the auspices of the Cleveland Probation Service whereby offenders nearing the end of a custodial sentence in a Young Offender Institution, can benefit from a range of courses and training programmes in the community. Offenders released into the community on a temporary basis receive help in relation to all the main problematic areas encountered by young people generally and not just offenders. These include how to survive in a bedsit, alcohol education, assertiveness training and welfare rights. The object is to re -integrate the offender into the community and to provide the necessary skills and support to reduce the likelihood of reoffending. What is particularly interesting is that though the scheme is an accepted element in the Cleveland alternatives programme, it is acknowledged that:

> "... we cannot justify the existence of temporary release on the basis of the scheme being effective at reducing the likelihood of reoffending".

Other criteria have to be employed and this serves to confirm the need to identify clearly what alternative objectives are being sought with community based measures.

The Dutch have also introduced a programme of Daily Custody (Dagdetentie, Ministrie de Justitie, 1991) in which long term prisoners, serving sentences of eight months or more may be detained in a hostel during the day but be allowed to go home to families and friends in the evening. The programme is, like so many other measures, built around the notion of constructive work. Offenders then are deprived of this liberty but do not lose contact with their family or community.

In relation to drug offenders, prisoners in Germany can also apply to the prosecutor for an interruption of sentence in favour of drug therapy in a community programme and this will be counted against the original sentence.

But it is in the development of community based measures as an option for sentencers that there has been perhaps the greatest expansion of resources in terms of both quantity and variety.

(b) Community Based Alternatives.

In both Scotland and England and Wales, the search for alternatives to custody has been promoted by the recognition of the inability of a prison sentence to reduce reoffending rates, the escalating cost of managing large prison populations, the benefits of community based approaches and through integration and co-ordination between the various statutory and voluntary services.

What also has to be remembered is that one of the most dramatic features of sentencing patterns in recent years has been the decline in the use of the fine. From 51% in 1977, the proportion of indictable offenders made the subject of a fine had fallen to 38% by 1987 (Home Office 1987). What also has to be said is that the decrease in the use of the fine cannot be attributed to the use of alternative monetary sanctions such as the compensation order but is seen as a response to the:

"*growth in unemployment and the difficulties in imposing a fine on people with low incomes (e.g. Crow and Simon 1987)*" (NACRO 1989a).

The concern is that the other community based measures may well be displacing the use of the fine, leaving the use of custodial sanctions largely unchanged.

Information about the use of other community based penalties, such as discharge (see NACRO 1989a) Community Service Orders (McIvor 1990) is readily accessible and though mention will be made of these, we intend to concentrate more on rather newer innovative measures in our review.

The nature that such programmes take will very often depend on the population targeted. For example, the development of measures for those with specific problems, drug or alcohol, has seen the growth of initiatives to meet the needs of such offenders. A good example of this would be the use of probation hostels such as the Allelon Hostel in Edinburgh for 16-21 year olds with alcohol related behavioural problems.

The Community Service Order has of course, been in use for some time and though behind developments in the UK, many countries in Europe are now progressing their community service strategies; a good example being the growth of the use of Travail dans l'Interet Generale in France (Aubusson de Cavarlay 1987). Being well established in this country, there are now a number of research reports on community service (McIvor 1990; Hoggarth 1991). The community service order is now an accepted part of sentencing policy though there is still some concern that the order may not be used as an alternative to prison but may be drawing on the population of offenders who may not have gone to prison anyway (Hoggarth 1991). Comment has already been made on the community service order in Chapter Two.

(c) Intensive Probation, Supervision and Related Schemes.

The Alternative to Custody programme in Dundee managed by the National Children's Home organisation has been heralded as a programme exhibiting all the requirements of a successful community based initiative. For the purposes of the review, the project is also particularly significant because the target population is the 16- 21 year old group.

The main aim of the NCH strategy in relation to young offenders is:

> "...to decrease the use of custody and increase the range of community disposals within the probation order, by designing individually tailored programmes, to meet the needs of this client group, within projects".

The Dundee project is the first of the NCH projects in Scotland partly modelled on the successful NCH ventures south of the border and operates on the philosophy that custody makes it more not less difficult for personal and social development which will have a more significant impact on reoffending rates. Committed to diverting young offenders from both prosecution and custody, the NCH Dundee project is only one of a number of schemes operated by the organisation in Scotland and is only one of a number of schemes throughout the UK in which diversion to an alternative to custody programme is part of a probation order.

In the Dundee project, referral to the programme either by the court or by the social worker writing the Social Enquiry Report, is as part of a probation order. The order will continue to be held by the supervising social worker and failure to follow the conditions of the order will result in breach conditions being implemented (see NCH leaflet). At all stages, the supervising social worker will liaise with project staff regarding the offender's entry to the scheme and progress during it.

Programmes are individually tailored and as well as addressing offence behaviour, the general problems experienced by young people, including those associated with drugs, alcohol, poor social skills and lack of knowledge about welfare rights are all tackled when appropriate.

A number of general comments can be made about the project itself and the way in which it reflects the working philosophy of those involved. (This can be read in reference to some of the general points made in the research literature discussed above).

Firstly, the programme, per capita, is much cheaper than custody.

Secondly, the project has gained from having established good working relationships between the agencies involved and the judiciary. This is reminiscent of the philosophy of the Rainer Foundation as discussed above and highlights the importance of close and meaningful contact between key actors in this contact. Examples given to illustrate the point included the extension in time given to the request for reports on potential referrals to the project and the fact that sheriffs themselves have visited and maintain contact with the project (Personal communication with J. Connolly, June 1991). Also, the High Court, not long after the establishment of the project, had referred a case, reflecting the belief that such a programme may be useful not simply for cases involving more minor offences (as other projects have suggested) but also for high tariff cases. The rapport, contact and negotiation between the sheriffs and those on the project is seen as testimony to the need for any programme to demonstrate credibility to sentencers.

Thirdly, the project had also been devised in reaction to a number of factors which were seen to inhibit the development of true alternatives and these included:

the lack of credible alternatives for consideration by fiscals and sentencers;

the poor quality of available disposals;

the lack of quality information available to the court at the time of sentencing;

the lack of consistent feedback for sentencers from social work and related programmes about the outcome of disposals; and

the reluctance of sheriffs to use community disposals in the absence of information or knowledge about the nature and efficacy about programmes.

The NCH programme is derived largely from the successful strategies already established in the Leeds Young Adult Offenders Project (see Brownlee 1990) as part of the Home Office Action Plan to set up intensive probation programmes exclusively for offenders who would otherwise receive custodial sentences. The Home Office has commissioned research to evaluate such intensive probation schemes in two areas and another on the introduction of intensive probation schemes in three urban areas. What all the intensive probation schemes have in common with the NCH project in Dundee is the tailoring of probation orders to the assessed needs of the individual. The main aims are to keep offenders in the community, to accept what they have done and to help resolve some of the practical problems experienced such as in the realm of housing, unemployment, etc.

The Dundee project, is in some sense, a case study in the management of these kinds of issues in the creation of an acceptable alternative to custody which galvanises the approach taken towards, and attitudes to dealing with young adult offenders. Once again, in comparing the NCH project with the alternative to custody project in Lothian where offenders as part of their probation order are required to attend the Pilton project, the significance of the management of the NCH programme by those who are neither part of the criminal justice system nor members of the Local Authority social work department has been identified as crucial. The NCH documents themselves point to their ability as an independent organisation to get services started quickly, to involve the community and to be innovative (see Chapter Two). The approach taken by the NCH generally is that of **working with** rather than **imposing something on**, and this reflects their practice both in working with young people and with formal authorities.

The NCH, however, have a number of other projects all of which can be said to make a contribution to keeping young people out of the criminal justice system and custody in particular. The Dumfries Community Project offers support to 12-16 year olds who have been before a children's hearing or who are returning to the community from residential care. The main aim is to prevent the reappearance of these children in the criminal justice and care systems. Similar objectives are set for their Clydesdale Youth Project. Their Stirling Stopover Project is exclusively for 16-21 year olds who are homeless and the Perth Youth Project is for 18-21 year olds who are encouraged to be independent and make good constructive use of their leisure time.

Another major organisation operating in Scotland and which has also established new programmes for young offenders is Save the Children Fund and their Dunbarton Project in particular is relevant for our purposes. Set up in 1988, the Dunbarton Project comprises two main programmes and teams. These are the Children's Hearings Team and the Sheriff Court Team.

The Children's Hearings Team was set up to work with those over 16 who are still in the Children's Hearings System and are at risk of entering the criminal justice system. Young people considered are those who are involved, or likely to become involved in offending and who need extra support and help to meet the problems posed by living in the community. It is also voluntary. Relating the programme to some of what we have already seen in the research literature, the scheme operates on the basis that the social context of the young person has to provide the opportunity for commitment, constructive use and direction of energy, the development of support structures and the ability to take risks.

Since the SCF project is also concerned to promote the notion of empowerment, of getting young people to recognise their responsibility for decisions in their lives, tension between the project and social workers is seen to result from the SCF team taking on an advocacy role in contrast to the more traditional approach taken by the local authority social workers. The team have also noted in this regard that some young people prefer to be passed on from the Hearings to the courts because it provides a possible release from social work supervision. Similarly, the problems posed by this age group for children's panel members will not be resolved, the team argues, by panel members continuing to believe that allowing offenders to go into the criminal justice system is a constructive way of handling these problems. Panel members as much as sheriffs may need to rethink their attitudes and approaches to this age group.

The Sheriff Court Team operates a similar approach and philosophy, working with those between 16 and 25 and though offence behaviour is an important element in their work, the team acknowledges that other factors in young people's lives, such as housing, jobs, etc., are just as important. What is particularly interesting is that the SCF sheriff court team has rejected group work as a means of working with young people. Rather, during the initial assessment, the young person reaches agreement as to what are the main priorities requiring to be tackled.

Group work is, however, seen to be an important vehicle for change in the Pilton Youth Project in Lothian where selected offenders, as part of their supervision or probation order, are required to attend. The focus is very much on the offending behaviour and peer group pressure is deployed in seeking to change it. The groups are not therapeutic since offending is not conceived as an illness but are educational and some concern is expressed that equivalent programmes in England and Wales are not sufficiently offence oriented.

Schemes similar to the NCH and the SCF ones in Scotland also operate in England and Wales. The Rainer Foundation, referred to already, also manages projects in London, Northamptonshire and Basingstoke and all are based on the need to keep offenders out of custody and to provide them with the personal skills and confidence to cope in the social world. They operate, generally in conjunction with local services and probation services, both a juvenile justice alternative to custody scheme and a young offenders alternative to custody scheme.

The Southend juvenile justice scheme was the first of eight alternative schemes for juveniles established by Rainer in Essex with the local authority and is unique in that unlike the others it is managed solely by the voluntary organisation itself. Providing individual programmes for young people between 14 and 17 who would otherwise have received custodial sentences, the scheme operates on the basis of close co-operation between local magistrates, Community Involvement Branch of the police as well as social services and prosecution. Indeed this form of close co-operation is a hallmark of the Rainer philosophy and failure in programmes is often attributed to a breakdown in, or failure to establish, good working relationships with others.

The value of the scheme to Essex has been clearly identified with a 50% reduction in the use of custody in the first year; with a reconviction rate of 59% for minor offences compared with the 85% associated with reconviction after custody. The involvement of the police had also seen a reduction in the number of actual prosecutions as a result of an increase in the use of police cautioning.

Of the young adult offender schemes operated by Rainer, The Kingsbury Project in Aylesbury is held up to be one of their most successful, exemplifying once again the importance of interagency working. Funded since March 1990, this is a joint initiative between the Buckinghamshire Probation Service and the Rainer Foundation. A good example of intensive probation work allied to the skills and expertise of the voluntary organisations, the Kingsbury project involves the Rainer team in working with the offender as regards employment and accommodation whilst the probation service offer a package which includes attendance at an offending behaviour group, individual offence counselling service, help with alcohol and drug related behaviour and so on.

The project is seen by all involved to be highly successful and the success is attributed to the close working relationships between the statutory services and between the statutory services and the voluntary sector. The project:

> *"epitomises a close partnership between a voluntary agency and the probation service.....the two agencies share the common objective of targeting high risk young offenders and there is constant dialogue between them".*

The failure of the Rainer Salford Project is conversely attributed to the breakdown in working relationships between the project and the probation service which continues to send young people only reluctantly.

In relation to juveniles, NACRO (1989), in monitoring the growth of local co-operation through the DHSS Initiative on Intermediate Treatment, has provided information on schemes to divert juveniles from custody in three local authority areas - in Westminster, Kent and Kirklees. The schemes in all three areas show a marked reduction in the use of custody and the report further argues that the initiative reduced care and custodial disposals by 50% between 1982 and 1987. Both the Home Office Action Plan and the DHSS IT initiative have had undoubted effect, for very similar reasons, on the use of custodial and related sanctions, but also on the nature of the working relationships between the different agencies involved.

The recognition of the importance of social, work and personal skills training has also influenced developments on the continent initially as with so many new initiatives, for juveniles but later in application to adults as a substitute for prison sentences of between 3 and 6 months (see in particular Dutch proposals for the development of skills training, De Whit 1991). Adults could be required to go to an attendance centre for anything up to 3 months. For young adult offenders, such programmes were seen to contain the potential for removing many from the criminal justice and ultimately the prison system and perhaps more so through the use of a combination of sanctions.

(d) Employment, Housing and Associated Areas.

What is obvious from the projects referred to so far is that employment and accommodation are issues of major concern for young people, whether offenders or not, and that many of the measures described include components designed to aid young adult offenders to solve, or at least cope with, housing, labour market and associated problems. Further, there is the general acceptance that any attempt to help young adult offenders **and** to reduce the numbers of those going into custody has to take into consideration the implications of low income, unsatisfactory accommodation and poor labour market possibilities.

The French (Bailleau 1990) employ the notion of "l'insertion" in reference to attempts to integrate the young into mainstream social life. By "l'insertion" is meant the philosophy of tackling all the aspects of a young person's life which is inhibiting them from participating in community and social life as fully as possible. Thus policies for dealing with young adults have to be related to the levels of income available to young people through income support policies. The French approach to the young is aided by the fact that, having recently adopted the policy of a minimum subsistence and income level, housing and other social policies in other areas are co-ordinated with the national incomes policy.

There is no such equivalent in the UK but the need to recognise the implications of such concerns is not only reflected in the development of strategies to deal with young offenders but also for young people generally in the interests of increasing their life opportunities and thereby inhibiting the level of risk to which they exposed themselves in a number of different areas in their lives. The integration of the young into the community requires more than just dealing with their offending behaviour.

In the UK, many of the measures and programmes premised on such considerations aim to target all sections of the youth population. For example, APEX has developed strategies to aid offenders, ex-offenders and young people at risk generally. In 1990, 2273 people called on the services of APEX and of these 45% were in the 16-20 age bracket (Annual Report 1990).

The main objective of the work of APEX is to give young offenders skills, information, support and confidence to enter the labour market. Working with employers, education and training institutions, the intention is to allow ex-offenders to achieve their rights in terms of the Rehabilitation of Offenders Act. Offenders are encouraged to accept responsibility both for their lives in general and for their offence behaviour. In that respect, the organisation operates as much on a philosophy of advocacy and empowerment as does the NCH and SCF projects. The Dundee and Dunbarton projects also have close working links with APEX when employment is seen to be a major issue for young offenders.

Amongst the young, APEX is seen to be particularly effective in that as an independent organisation, project workers are not associated with formal institutions like social work and school. Moreover, as a voluntary programme, participation is a matter of choice, not of compulsion. One of the major merits of the programme over more statutory based measures is that consistency in acceptance and in support is offered to a client group many of whom have lacked an element of consistency throughout their lives.

In a review of the programmes under the auspices of their foundation, the Eisenhower Foundation (Annual Report 1990 and personal communication with the Director, July 1991) in the USA could forcefully assert that their programmes do reduce recidivism and that the cost per youth involved was almost half that of prisons in comparison to residential programs and even less for non-residential programmes. The Eisenhower Foundation operates on the philosophy, in complete rejection of the Martinson thesis that nothing works, that we do know how to prevent at risk young adults adopting a criminal career. The Eisenhower programmes involve a variety of measures and combinations of these but include the Job Corps nationally (intensive job support training); the Argus Community; the Fairview Homes Public Housing crime prevention programme (tenant empowerment and employment of high risk youth); Jobstart (high school completion among disadvantaged drop outs between 17 and 21); and Project Redirection (involving better employment opportunities for disadvantaged teenage mothers of 17 or younger).

The Eisenhower Foundation can attribute its success in reducing the crime and drug involvement of young adults to a number of factors including the ability of non profit or voluntary organisations to manage programmes and the fact that programmes are realistically resourced and staff are well trained and skilled. The use of volunteers was seen to militate against successful implementation of programmes. The role of the police is also a crucial variable as for other public, statutory services.

The work of NACRO, though less ambitious than the Eisenhower strategy, through the Youth Activity Unit projects in deprived areas aimed at making constructive use of youth leisure time (Wolverhampton YAU and Nottingham YAU) and helping with employment matters (Henley Green) have also provided a model for a number of similar ventures in England and Wales. NACRO too are confident that such projects make a substantial contribution to the reduction of crime in the housing estates as well as indirectly to the well being of the community as a whole (NACRO Youth Activities Unit 1990b).

The main point to draw from this section is that any attempt to deal with young adult offenders which ignores the effects of employment and its relationship to the general life opportunities of young people will have a poorer chance of success. The work of APEX, NACRO and related organisations cannot in themselves provide a comprehensive strategy to deal with all the factors which promote criminal behaviour.

Nevertheless, they and the Eisenhower Foundation do point to the way in which the behaviour of young people is seriously circumscribed by the social, economic and political conditions in which they live and that any attempt to prevent criminal behaviour may then have to tackle these factors on a wider front. Solutions to the difficulties experienced and posed by young adults may well require multiple solutions involving widespread agency co-operation. This may in itself require a youth strategy or youth policy in which different agencies not only work together in collaboration but are also governed by a co-ordinated policy framework.

In the following section we will consider the possibilities offered to the reduction of crime by young people through social crime prevention programmes.

(e) Crime Prevention and Social Crime Prevention.

Though criticism has often been directed at the failure of the UK to develop meaningful post-sentence measures as alternatives to custody, it has to be said that in general, European countries have made even less progress in this context. Where most European countries have invested most of their effort in recent years has been in the promotion of social crime prevention strategies, particularly along the lines of the French system. In terms of the distinctions drawn by Smith and Gill (1989, p40), most European countries have concentrated more on primary intervention (including community development and broad strategies to reduce the incidence or likelihood of crime) and less on secondary and tertiary programmes.

A clear distinction has to be made between recent trends in crime prevention and in social crime prevention.

There are currently 148 crime prevention panels distributed throughout Scotland and almost 2000 Neighbourhood Watch schemes. Though there are attempts to prevent crime through education strategies etc., for the most part such schemes involve a policy of target hardening and have focused more on situational rather than social factors. That in itself is perhaps not difficult to understand given the difficulty of identifying those social factors involved and in devising appropriate policies.

Although there are, of course, attempts to have different agencies collaborate in a crime prevention strategy, this does not mean quite the same thing as the form of co-ordinated, integrated policy envisaged within a social crime prevention approach. What crime prevention panels have done is to include more and more people from outwith the criminal justice system in the attempt to deal with criminal behaviour and have emphasised the inability of the criminal justice system alone to deal with offenders and the causes of crime (Graham 1990).

This has meant that gradually the relationship between criminal policy and social policies has had to be continually reappraised and readjusted in order to accommodate housing, incomes, education, employment and youth policies in the search for a solution to the problems posed by criminal behaviour, particularly by the young adult. For this reason, the association of the police with the crime prevention panels is seen to inhibit the growth of a true social crime prevention strategy (Gill, interview 1991).

Social crime prevention can be taken as the attempt to solve the problems of criminal behaviour by tackling the root causes of crime and may be best described as primary prevention as the notion is employed by Graham (1990).

Primary prevention refers to those attempts to influence crime producing situations through social, economic and other areas of social policy. Since the section of the population most at risk in deprived and socially disadvantaged areas are young adults then social crime prevention is seen as particularly important in inhibiting the growth of crime amongst this age group by ameliorating the conditions in which they and other groups of young people at risk find themselves.

Most European countries have confirmed that a policy of social crime prevention is currently either being devised or put into operation. The best known example of a social crime prevention policy is of course that arising from the Bonnemaison Report of France. Pierre de Liege (1991) and King (1988) give a good account of the formulation and implementation of the social crime prevention policy in France and since most similar policies are based on it, it is worth briefly identifying its key characteristics.

Social crime prevention rests on the following principles:

individualistic explanations of crime are rejected as the only form of explanation. Social, economic and political factors also have to be taken into account;

traditional hard line and punitive approaches have been shown to have involved a considerable waste of public money with little effect on crime rates;

criminal policies must be devised with reference to other social strategies;

adequate resources should be provided for a realistic implementation of a social crime prevention policy;

these resources should be devolved to local authority level since there can be no national template that applies to all parts of the country. Attempts to combat rising crime rates amongst the young and to meet the variety of problems they both experience and pose have to be developed at the local level. Fiscal devolution is also accompanied by the power to determine the social crime prevention strategy **within** the community involved;

as far as possible, those in the community are to be involved in determining the nature of the strategy formulated.

What has to be remembered is that the French formulation of a social crime prevention policy was determined in part by the wish to devolve power from the centre to the regional level. The search for a new approach was governed by the failure of traditional hard line measures to deal with the problems increasingly posed by the young whose criminal activities were seen to derive from their alienation and marginalisation from the opportunities offered to others in society.

Nevertheless, concern at rising crime rates throughout Europe, particularly in the knowledge that increased expenditure on crime control policies appeared to have little effect on the rate of crime, has driven the search for radical alternatives. For that reason, the "French alternative" King (1988) was readily accepted as the model for a number of European countries including Hungary (Gonzcol 1989) and Holland (Fijnault 1992).

Garapon (Interview, Paris 1991) could confidently assert that in the Creteil area of Paris served by the court in which he was a magistrate, crime rates had gone down by at least 50% since the introduction of a social crime prevention strategy in the area.

Strathclyde's policy on young people, set out in Working with Young People (1984) and Working with Young People at Risk (1985) has been characterised by Smith and Gill (1989) as a social crime prevention programme and the nearest British approach to the Bonnemaison ideals. Nevertheless, though the Strathclyde approach does show interagency co-operation at both policy and practice level, it does not have the fully integrated framework of the other major British social crime prevention initiative - the Community Safety Strategy of Birmingham.

In the Community Safety Strategy in Birmingham, elements of the French philosophy are obvious - the criminal justice system has very little impact on the crime committed in communities; concern is with the social not just individual explanations of crime; and the basis of the policy is to address the question not of how to deal with criminal behaviour but what kind of city should Birmingham be.

Within the policy adopted, a diverse number of measures and strategies are implemented all of which are co-ordinated at the policy level. For example, the measures include community based projects, inner city partnerships (much like the Eisenhower Foundation); crime within the school curriculum, projects on drug abuse, projects on altering the physical environment of the city (for example, ridding the city of the notorious Birmingham underpasses). Co-ordination at the policy level is guaranteed by the fact that all local authority departments have to show that they are making a contribution to community safety in their plans or forfeit part of their budget.

Local representation is ensured through crime prevention panels and task groups with a direct input into the formulation and implementation of the community safety strategy. The local element as envisaged in the Bonnemaison approach is ensured. However, in commenting on the wider context in which the Birmingham community safety project operates, Sinclair (1992) asserts the need for local strategies to be aided by national economic policies which did not undermine the social objectives of local initiatives.

In particular, again very like the French approach, what came under attack was the continued willingness of governments to invest more money in law enforcement strategies and custodial institutions and to under-resource alternative initiatives; and also, the way in which policies governing housing, housing benefit, employment and incomes policies had in themselves contributed to the situation and circumstances with which local authorities were asked to deal. In relation to the latter, were those policies which were seen to contribute to increased homelessness amongst young adults at a time of reduced labour market possibilities.

Nor is Birmingham the only source registering concern on such issues with the Association of Metropolitan Authorities criticising the lack of comprehensive strategies and, in relation to crime prevention specifically, the concentration of criminal policy on "short-term, situational and project based activities" (1990). The Association of London Authorities also made similar comments (1990) about the need for a corporate approach and, as regards young offenders, urges the establishment of Joint Education, Leisure and Recreation sub-committees to promote policies for young people in general. NACRO (1991b) has also supplemented its demands for an interagency strategy with a request for wider support for children, families and young people.

It is, of course, too early to make any realistic comment on the long-term outcome of such strategies as implemented under the banner of social crime prevention. France has set up a research programme designed specifically to evaluate the social crime prevention programmes in 30 or so 'departements'.

Nevertheless, what has to be taken from the ready acceptance of this approach is that there is a willingness to consider radical alternatives in the search for measures which will have a long-term effect on crime rates and more generally on the life chances of young people. It also has to be seen as part of a move towards redefining criminal behaviour, its causes and the solutions to it. The difficulty that this presents is that it will add to the current confusion and lack of clarity as to the purposes and objectives of the criminal justice system and its relationship to other social policies. If the result is the adoption or establishing of a rational framework for crime control then that in itself would surely be of considerable benefit. At this juncture, however, some time may pass before the long-term outcomes themselves of such a strategy can become clear.

Chapter Four

Young Adult Offenders - Issues and Way Forward

Main Issues

Young adult offenders pose particular problems for criminal justice systems because their behaviour and experiences intersect with many other policy considerations. Most of the developments throughout Europe are based on the recognition that this age group experiences additional difficulties in social integration because of the transition from school to work, the rigours of the labour market, family problems and a number of other factors associated with low income. For that reason, attempts to deal with the young adult offender have crystallised the complexity of integrating criminal policies with other social policies, and of articulating the relationship between criminal justice and social justice.

For that reason also, it has to be said that there are few measures or strategies being adopted which apply specifically to young adult offenders. Rather, the development of measures has been in relation to offenders generally and some of these are seen to have particular merit for young adults.

In this chapter, we intend to look at the main issues that can be drawn from the available research, from a statement of available measures and programmes, and from the discussions held and contacts made during the course of this short review. In the final section, this will then be employed in making a number of suggestions for future developments.

(i) **Funding and Resources.**

The provision of adequate funding for the development of strategies for young adult offenders is, of course, a crucial issue for all attempts to provide effective measures. But with specific reference to the Scottish context, the matter has particular relevance in reference to the issue of 100% funding.

Considerable concern is expressed that the 100% funding arrangements, by being targeted on those who are in the criminal justice system, will inhibit local authorities and others in the development of appropriate strategies for tackling crime. In particular, the concern is that measures will be devised more in response to resource provision than to needs and that this will have particular implications for the development of measures for young offenders and for youth policies generally.

For example, members of the Association of Directors of Social Work (Seminar, 1991) have expressed concern that young offenders will be diverted from the

Children's Hearings System into the criminal justice system because of 100% funding and that there will be a policy of up-tariffing offence cases to benefit from the 100% funding arrangements. A number of implications follow from this.

One is obviously concern that more, rather than less young offenders in the 16-18 age group will go through the criminal justice system because of the financial implications. This is in contrast to the proposal made in the Child Care Law Review and to developments in Europe where consideration is given and being given, to extending the remit of the juvenile justice system to include older categories of offenders. It has to be said, however, that not all see the 100% funding arrangements in this light since, given the absence of resources in the Children's Hearings System, it may be preferable to send older offenders to the criminal justice system because it is and will be better resourced because of these arrangements.

There is also concern that the funding of post sentence arrangements will inhibit the growth of pre-trial diversionary strategies such as mediation.

The new arrangements could also have an inhibiting effect on the development of preventive strategies since they do not come under the 100% funding arrangements. Moreover, this is seen to be problematic not just for the statutory agencies but also for the voluntary bodies, such as SACRO, whose preventive work would be seriously restricted. Given the drive towards some form of social crime prevention, it is not clear to key actors just where the money would come from.

(ii) Juvenile justice and Criminal Justice Interface.

We have already argued that any examination of measures for young adults has to be seen in relation to what happens with juvenile offenders. It is, in our view, impossible to dissociate juvenile justice strategies from the long term objectives of reducing the number of young people who go through the criminal justice system. This is no more true than at the interface between the two systems at a time when, in Europe, there is a drive in a number of countries to increase the jurisdiction of the juvenile justice system for older age groups and to replicate for adults many of the measures tried and tested for children.

All countries contacted during the project indicated the problems associated with the relationship between the criminal justice and the juvenile justice systems. No matter the variety of age ranges and the different legislative frameworks, the transition from the one to the other generally posed difficulties and this is to be expected since the overlap is not purely practical but is based on very different ideologies of crime and crime control.

Nevertheless, the transition from the Hearings System to the criminal justice system is seen by some European commentators to be particularly harsh. In relation to the above discussion, the 100% funding arrangements may well militate against increased us of options already available under current legislation.

For example, 16, 17 and 17 and a half year olds can, under the present legislative arrangements, be retained within the Hearings System though it appears that very few are. This has to be qualified by pointing to the diversity of practice throughout Scotland with certain regions identified as dealing with many 16 and 17 year olds in the Hearings System (in the Grampian area) and others with very few (for example, Edinburgh). (Sheriff in interview, 1991).

What are the factors which inhibit the use of such arrangements as apply at present? Why are existing arrangements not often used? The discussion in the section above suggests that the lack of resources could well be a factor though others have suggested that panel members do not feel that hearings are the appropriate forum for deciding on how to deal with young adults. Yet most of the evidence suggests that many young adult offenders commit fairly trivial offences but that the consequences of appearance in the criminal justice system (in terms of criminal career development) may far outweigh the seriousness of what they have done.

More information on the factors that inhibit use of the existing legislation is surely required and would be beneficial in any long term appraisal of how to deal with young adults between 16 and 18.

(iii) Interagency Co-operation.

One of the key variables that has been identified as having a significant impact on the success or otherwise of measures is the extent to which there is interagency co-operation. The idea of interagency collaboration was a feature of official and other documents in the late 1980's and in practice it has proved to be a vital component in both the formulation and implementation of policies for offenders generally and young offenders in particular. A number of points can be made.

Firstly, voluntary agencies are seen to play a significant role in the establishment of measures and programmes for young adult offenders. Rainer, NCH, Save the Children and others in Europe have all been identified as being able to offer an approach which statutory agencies cannot offer. In particular, the voluntaries are more flexible and innovative in their ideas and working practices; they are less associated by the young with formal authority and they can act as a galvanising force for the deployment of local resources in a way that statutory authorities are unable to do.

Also, it is generally accepted that tackling the offending behaviour of young adults is inappropriate without recognising the kinds of problems they typically face and which may contribute to their offending behaviour. For that reason, the criminal justice system can benefit greatly by being involved with those voluntary agencies which have as their concern: housing, employment and related issues.

Secondly, the probation service in particular amongst the statutory agencies in England and Wales has resisted cooperation with the voluntaries, largely because of the threat to the role they had traditionally played in relation to dealing with offenders. As we have seen, a number of commentators have attributed the failure of projects to the inability or reluctance of the probation service to co-operate in collaborative ventures for young offenders. The absence of a separate probation service in Scotland is seen (NCH, interview 1991) to be a positive factor because of the clearer association between working with offenders and working with those in need of support, help, care, etc. The general point to be made is that interagency cooperation is a crucial variable and that the voluntary organisations have a vital role to play in the development of constructive and effective strategies.

Thirdly, but closely tied in with the last point is the fact that close collaboration and contact is required between the service organisations and the judiciary. What the NCH project and others (Carnie 1990) have identified is the way in which this close collaboration, even prior to the establishing of a project, is both important in terms of its potential success but is also welcomed by members of the judiciary who are then better informed about the measures available as alternatives to custody. Related to this is also the acceptance by sentencers of the benefits of the introduction of National Standards, particularly in allowing sentencers to have forewarning of what they can now expect to happen, for example, on a probation order.

Fourthly, collaboration with the judiciary is more easily attained when there are clear grounds for credibility of the measure. In this respect, what is obviously just as important as the content of programmes and projects is the quality of the service provision. Well trained, experienced staff is high on the priority for a number of the organisations involved in the provision of measures for offenders and there is an increasing reluctance to use volunteers and ill experienced personnel.

Fifthly, sentencers lack clear guidelines and appropriate information bases on which to draw to aid them in sentencing young adult offenders. We shall return to this in the concluding section. There is, however, some evidence to suggest that clear guidelines could be particularly helpful in reducing the numbers of young adults given custodial sentences. These could only operate effectively within a framework of realistically resourced alternatives.

Lastly, and again related to the foregoing discussion, the collaboration between agencies is made simpler and the effectiveness of measures more assured where there is a clear statement of purpose. The danger of combined orders is that they introduce too many conflicting objectives and involve too many diverse groups.

(iv) Social Crime Prevention.

True social crime prevention strategies, where they are to be implemented, have to move away from a target hardening approach focusing on situational aspects of crime and have to develop a corporate approach to tackle fundamental social and economic factors which contribute to the production of criminal behaviour and the general reduction of life opportunities for the young.

Social crime prevention strategies have to be located within a framework which allows for local and regional initiatives to be formulated and implemented within national policies. What is noteworthy at this stage is that though such strategies require a major re-think on the nature of crime and its causation and a new approach to resource planning and distribution, there is evidence to suggest that the individualistic explanations of crime are being abandoned throughout Europe and that societal explanations and collective solutions are becoming increasingly acceptable to the man in the street.(Farrell and Heidensohn 1991).

The Way Forward

The significance of interagency collaboration is by now obvious in developing measures for young adult offenders. Nevertheless, we believe that there are still considerable obstacles and barriers to meaningful collaboration, mainly due to:

the maintenance of competing and conflicting ideologies about how to deal with young adults; and

the lack of information by key actors in the criminal justice process and in related agencies about just what members of other organisations are seeking or hope to achieve.

Collaboration has to mean more than simply close proximity in working relationships and has to mean the sharing of key assumptions and ideas about initiatives. For that reason, **we recommend that consideration be given to the establishment of, or at least encouragement for, some form of interdisciplinary seminars, workshops or meetings held at a local, regional or national level to allow members of different professions, including the judiciary, to discuss the difficulties and problems from the perspectives of the different constituencies involved in dealing with young adult offenders.**

Such an approach could be adopted at different levels, involving policy makers or practitioners, statutory or voluntary agencies, or some mixture of these and could contribute both to the development of an agreed policy meeting the requirements of specific areas within the constraint of local authority and other financial considerations.

Certainly, despite the trend towards interagency collaboration, there did appear from both the literature and contact with key actors during our review, to be a fair amount of disagreement and misunderstanding in relation to dealing with young adults. This could well be because the shifts in policy have very often been for pragmatic reasons and there has been little attempt to devise a coherent policy, or more importantly, a coherent philosophy to underpin such trends. Researchers could well be involved as catalysts and facilitators in such an exercise.

In relation to possible research in the future, a number of suggestions can be made.

Because of the scope of a review that lasted only six months, little information, other than broad generalisations, was collected on the nature of the offences committed by young adults. **We suggest that a proper statistical analysis be conducted of the kinds of offences committed by young adults and how these are dealt with in the criminal justice system.** This would provide an important baseline on which to ground the development of policies for young offenders, particularly when the issue of targeting either specific types of offenders or offences has to be taken into consideration. More realistic comparisons could be drawn between UK practices and information contained in European databases.

We also recommend that more information be sought on the nature of the criminal careers of young adult offenders. Again, lack of information on the delinquent and criminal careers of young adults inhibits the realistic development of measures to meet the problems experienced and posed by this particular age group. The rejection of all embracing explanations of criminal behaviours has to be supplemented by appropriate information on which to base policies and to devise measures. It may be that the work by Kinsey et al. (1991) could be developed in this respect.

We also suggest that consideration be given to producing more information on sentencing decisions in order to elicit what use is being made of community based alternatives, but more importantly, for what reasons.

In addition, **information could be sought on the reasons and factors which account for the apparent reluctance of children's panel members to retain 16, 17 and 17 and a half year olds.** The numbers going to custody from the criminal justice system could well be reduced with a more liberal use of the existing legislative arrangements.

In terms of evaluation of key strategies, **we recommend that significant projects such as the NCH Dundee project or the Rainer initiatives in England and Wales, be evaluated fully because of the potential they have in providing a model for other developments.** In the absence of research, such measures could be the subject of continual monitoring for information purposes.

Research into the implementation of a social crime prevention strategy would of course be a costly exercise, particularly if such a strategy had to be instituted in the first place. Nevertheless, given the significance of this approach and its acceptability throughout Europe and in North America, we consider that it would be important to continue to monitor the long-term achievements of social crime prevention. We suggest that **a monitoring exercise be undertaken, of either the 30 research projects established in France or of the progress of the Community Safety Project in Birmingham.** This could involve little cost but could provide extremely useful information for consideration in policy formulation.

References and Bibliography

Andrews, D.A. and Keissling, J.J. (1980)   *Program structure and effective correctional practices: A summary of the CaVIC research,* in Ross RR and Gendreau P. Effective Correctional Treatment, Toronto: Butterworths.

Andrews, D. A. et al. (1986)   The risk principle of case classification: An outcome evaluation with young adult probationers,*Canadian Journal of Criminology,* 28, 377-84.

A.D.S.W. (1991)   *Young Offenders, the Criminal Justice System and the Children's Hearings System.*

A.M.A. (1990)   *Crime Reduction : A Framework for the Nineties?*

Aubusson de Cavarlay, B. (1987)   La Diversite de traitement penale, *Donnees Sociales,* 8, pp 589-593.

Baechtold, E. (1988)   *Young Adult Offenders, in Prison.* Information Bulletin,Council of Europe.

Bailleau, F. (1991)   *La Coordination des Services dans les Domaines Sociales,* Council of Europe, CDEM (91) 1.

Bailleau, F. and Garioud, G. (1990)   *New Social Strategies and the Criminal Justice System*, Council of Europe, PC-CRC(90) 12

Baldcock, J. (1980)   Why the prison population has grown larger and younger , *Howard Journal,*19, 142-155.

Barkwell, L. (1976)   Differential treatment of juveniles on probation: An evaluative study, *Canadian Journal of Criminology*, 18, 363-78.

Barkwell, L. (1980)   *Differential probation treatment of delinquency,* in R.R.Ross and P. Gendreau, (eds.) Effective Correctional Treatment, Toronto: Butterworths.

Bennett- Emslie,G., McClintock, D., Robertson, A., van Teijlingen E., and Wade, E. (1990)

Intermediate Treatment in Scotland , University of Edinburgh.

Van Boogart, H.

The Creation of the Non-Divertible, in Hudson and Galaway op. cit.

Brody, S. R. (1976)

The Effectiveness of Sentencing: A Review of the Literature , Home Office Research Study, no. 35.

Brownlee, I. (1990)

Targetting the Young Adult Offender: an evaluation project in Leeds, in *Criminal Law Review.*

Carnie, J. (1990)

Sentencers' Perceptions of Community Service by Offenders, Edinburgh: CRU.

De Cauter, F. (1991)

The Commission of Mediation for Special Youth Assistance, xerox.

Council of Europe. (1980)

Decriminalisation , Strasbourg.

Creamer, A., Hartley, L. and Williams, B. (1992)

The Probation Alternative: a study of the Impact of four Enhanced Probation Schemes on Sentencing Outcomes CRU, The Scottish Office.

Curtis, L. (1992)

Initiatives in the United States, in *Crime and Social Policy,* NACRO, London.

Ditton, J. et al.(1989)

Probation in Scotland: A Synthesis of Findings, Criminology Research Unit, University of Glasgow.

Dongier, S. and Dooselaere, D. (1991)

Approaching Mediation in Juvenile Court, xerox.

Dunkel, F. (1990)

Experience de Mediation in Republique Federale d'Allemagne, Les Experience de Mediation, Protection Judiciaire de la Jeunesse, Paris.

Dunkel, F. (1991)

Legal Differences in Europe Relevant to Juvenile Criminology, xerox.

Eisenhower Foundation .(1990)

Youth Investment and Community Reconstruction, Annual Report.

Evans, R and Wilkinson, C. (1990)

Young Adult Offenders in North-hamptonshire, Report to HORS.

Farrell and Heidensohn. (1991)

Crime in Europe, London, Routledge.

Faugeron, C. (1991)

La Production de L'ordre et Le Controle Penale , *Deviance et Societe*, Vol 15, No. 1, pp 51-91.

Faugeron, C. and Houchon, G.(1987)

Prison and the Penal System , the *International Journal of the Sociology of Law,* 15, pp 393-422.

Feest, J. (1988)

Reducing the Prison Population: Lessons from the West German Experience?, London, NACRO.

Feest, J. (1990)

New Social Strategies and the Criminal Justice System, Council of Europe, PC-CRC(90) ,14.

Fijnault, C. (1992)

The Disconnection of Social Policy and Crime in the Netherlands, *Crime and Social Policy,* London, NACRO.

Fischer, D. and Jeune, R .(1987)

Juvenile Diversion: a process analysis, *Canadian Psychology,* 28, pp 60-70.

Folkard, M.S. et al. (1974)

IMPACT vol. I : The Design of the Probation Experiment and an Interim Evaluation, Home Office Research Study, no. 36, London, HMSO.

Folkard, M.S. et al. (1976)

IMPACT vol. II: The Results of the Experiment, Home Office Research Study, no. 36,London, HMSO.

Gendreau, P. and Ross, R.R. (1987)

Revivification of rehabilitation: Evidence from the 1980s, *Justice Quarterly,* 4 , 349-407.

Gill, K. and Pickles, T. (1989)

Active Collaboration: Joint Practice And Youth Strategies, ITRC, Glasgow.

Gonzcol, K. (1989)

Reducing the prison population in Hungary, xerox.

Gonzcol, K. (1992)

Crime and Crime Prevention in Hungary at the Time of the Change in Regime,*Crime and Social Policy,* NACRO, London.

Gordon, D. A. and Arbuthnott, J. (1987)

Individual, group and family interventions, H.C. Quay (ed.) Hand-book of Juvenile Delinquency, New York, Wiley.

Gottschalk, R. et al.(1987)

Community- based interventions, in H. C. Quay.(ed.) Handbook of Juvenile Delinquency, New York, Wiley.

Graham, J. (1990)

Crime Prevention Strategies in Europe and North America, Helsinki, HEUNI.

Hessmer, H. (1989)

Tackling the Conflict; a framework analysis for Dispute Settlement, in Hudson and Galaway op. cit.

Hickey, C. and Douglas C. (1989)

Bail Out Support Scheme, Jan-Dec 1988, The Rainer Foundation.

Hoggarth, E. (1991)

Selection for Community Service Orders, Aldershot, Avebury.

Home Office (1987)

Crime Statistics for England and Wales, Table 3.7.

Home Office (1988a)

Punishment, Custody and the Community, Cm. 424.

Home Office (1988b)

Tackling Offending: an action plan, London, Home Office.

Home Office (1990)

Crime Justice and Protecting the Public, Cm. 965.

Hudson,J.and Galaway B.(eds.) (1989)

The State as Parent, NATO.

Hurley, N. (1987)

A Need to be Counted, Edinburgh: APEX.

Jardine et al.(1983)

Community Service Orders, employment and the tariff, in *Criminal Law Review*, pp 17-20.

Joutsen, M. (1991)

Fax communication.

Kimberly, P.and Peachey, D. (1991)

Face to Face: Victim Offender Mediation under the Young Offenders Act, xerox.

King, M. (1988)

The French Experience: How to make Social Crime Prevention work, London, NACRO.

Lipton, D. et al.(1975)

Effectiveness of Correctional Treatment: A Survey of Treatment Evaluation Studies, Springfield, Praeger.

Lockyer, A. (1989)

Study of Children's Hearings' Disposals in Relation to Resources, Children's Panel Chairmen's Group.

McIvor, G . (1989)
An Evaluative Study of Community Service by Offenders in Scotland, Social Work Research Centre, University of Stirling.

McIvor, G. (1990)
Sanctions for Serious or Persistent Offenders: Review of the Literature, Social Work Research Centre, University of Stirling.

Mackay, R. (1988)
Reparation in Criminal Justice, SACRO, Edinburgh.

Mair, G. (ed.) (1989 a)
Risk Prediction and Probation: Papers from a Research and Planning Unit Workshop , RPU, Paper 56, Home Office.

Mair, G. (1989 b)
Some developments in probation in the 1980's, RPU Research Bulletin no.27, 33- 36?

Mair, G (1991 a)
Controlling Young Adult Offenders in the Community : Sernor Attendance Centres and Day Centres, in McNeill and Williams (eds.) Containing Crime: Community based approaches, (University of Aberdeen Press).

Mair, G. (1991b)
Measuring the effectiveness of sentences, RPU Research Bulletin.

Marshall, T.and Merry, S. (1990)
Agressions Conflit in Paris, SOS.

Marshall, T. and Merry, S. (1990)
Crime and Accountability, London, Home Office.

Marshall, T. and Walpole,M. (1985)
Bringing People Together, HORS, No 33.

Mason, P. (1991)
Support Strategies in Inside Juvenile Justice, Community Care.

Millar, A. and Stedward, G. (1989)
Diversion from Prosecution- Vol 1. Diversion to Social Work. CRU, Edinburgh.

Ministerie van Justitie.(1991)
The Halt Programme, xerox.

Dagdetentie Project. (1991)
Project Leaflet.

Moxon, D. (1988)
Sentencing Practice in the Crown Court, HORS, No 103.

NACRO.(1989)

Replacing Custody: Findings from Two Census Surveys of Schemes for Juvenile Offenders Funded under the DHSS IT Initiative.

NACRO.(1989a)

The Real Alternative: Strategies to promote community based penalties.

NACRO.(1990)

Criminal Justice Policy for the 1990s: A Response to the Government's White Paper 'Crime, Justice and Protecting the Public'.

NACRO.(1990a)

Youth Activities Unit, Brochure.

NACRO.(1991)

Criminal Justice Bill 1990: Implications for Juveniles and Young Adult Offenders.

NACRO.(1991a)

Preventing Youth Crime, Report no. 3 .

Pease, K., Billingham, S. and Earnshaw, I. (1977)

Community service assessed in 1976, Home Office Research Study no. 39, London, HMSO.

Pelikan, C. (1990)

The Austrian Juvenile Justice Act, 1988, xerox.

Pelikan, C. (1991)

Conflict Resolution between Victims and Offenders in Austria and in the Federal Republic of Germany, in Heidensohn and Farrell, op. cit.

Plewig, H. (1989)

Law Policies and Implications for the YouthWelfare System: the Hamburg Example, in Hudson and Galaway, op cit.

Pratt, J. (1986)

Diversion from the Juvenile Court, in British Journal of Criminology, Vol 26, No. 3 July.

The Rainer Foundation (1990),

Salford Young Adult Offenders Project: Report to the Home Office 1/11/89- 31/5/90.

The Rainer Foundation(1991)

The Kingsbury Project: Report to the Home Office 1/3/90- 1/3/91.

Raynor, P. (1988)

Probation as an Alternative to Custody, Aldershot, Avebury.

Roberts, C.H. (1989)   *Hereford and Worcester Probation Service Young Offenders Project : First Evaluation Report,* Department of Social and Administration Studies, University of Oxford.

Rutherford, A. (1984)   *Prisons and the Process of Justice,* London.

Sarnecki, J. (1991)   *Juvenile Delinquency in Sweden,* National Council for Crime Prevention.

Sinclair, C. (1992)   Community Safety Project in Birmingham, *Crime and Social Policy,* London, NACRO.

Sinclair, J. (1991)   *Probation Hostels* (xerox available).

Smith, D. and Gill, K. (1989)   Young People and Social Crime Prevention in Scotland, *Youth and Policy,* no. 27.

SWSG .(1990)   *National Guidelines on Diversion to Social Work Agencies as an Alternative to Prosecution.*

SWSG. (1991)   *National Objectives and Standards for Social Work Services in the Criminal Justice System.*

Spencer, J. (1973)   *The Young Adult Offender,* Sophie Boyd Memorial Lecture, Toronto University.

Stanley, C. (1990)   *The French Alternative: Delinquency and Child Protection in France,* London, NACRO.

Stone, C. (1988)   *Final report on the Probation Initiative "Diversion from Custody and Prosecution",* London.

Strathclyde Regional Council (1984)   *Working with Young People.*

Strathclyde Regional Council (1985)   *Working with young People at Risk.*

United Nations (1989)   *Report of the International Seminar on the Prevention and Treatment of Juvenile Delinquency through Community Participation,* TCD/SEM 89/4.

Vestergard, J. (1991)   *Juvenile Contracting in Denmark,* xerox.

Walgrave, L., Welzeniz, I. and Berx, E. — *Dealing with Young Adult Offenders in Belgium*, xerox.

Warner, S. (1992) — *Making Amends: Justice for Victims and Offenders,* Evaluative Studies in Social Work, No 4, Avebury.

Whitehead,P., Turver,N and Wheatley, J. (1991) — *Probation,Temporary Release Schemes and Reconviction*, Aldershot, Avebury.

Wikstrom, P. (ed.) (1991) — *Crime and Measures Against Crime in the City,* National Council for Crime Prevention, Sweden.

Part 2

Criminal Justice and Related Services for Young Adult Offenders

Gender Issues

Elaine Samuel

Introduction

Given the broad scope of the Review of Criminal Justice and Related Services for Young Adult Offenders described in Part 1 and the constraints of its six month term, a comprehensive review was never envisaged, and the development of several lines of enquiry had to be ignored - amongst them, gender related issues. This was justified by the numbers of young men caught up in the criminal justice system in Scotland compared to young women, and not because issues raised by the research, or because all policy and practice recommendations, appeared to be identical for young males and females. Since 33 times as many young male offenders were received into penal establishments under sentence than young women in Scotland in 1990, the urgency with which new measures are required to reduce the large and disproportionately high number of offenders between 16 and 21 in Scottish prisons had to be treated, for the purposes of the Review, as a largely male affair.

It was also justified by the fact that crime is "overwhelmingly a male activity" (Morris 1987) and particularly, it may added, for those crimes most condemned or feared. Burglary, sexual assault, robbery and violence were identified by the British Crime Survey (Mayhew et al.1989) to be of greatest concern to the public and yet, on the basis of those apprehended, they are least likely to be committed by women. Crimes for which females are most likely to be charged, such as theft from shops or fraud and forgery, are perceived to be mainly at the expense of institutions and not identifiable members of the general public. They have therefore not been taken up with the same sense of urgency.

Because female offenders neither place an unbearable burden on the prison service and public purse nor constitute a public threat, issues specific to female offenders are often ignored and obscured. Though our Review is couched in gender neutral language, for example, it is concerned not so much with all young offenders but mainly with young male offenders - even if much of what is written about males may apply to females as well. What is problematic, then, is that what is applicable to both- and what is **not** applicable to both - is never specified. It may be argued that by writing about young male offenders **as if** all young offenders were included, young female offenders have been written out of the Review, as well as out of any subsequent development in research or practice generated by it.

This is common to much of the criminology and penology literature reviewed for the project and, with the notable exception of the academic feminist criminology literature which emerged in the late 1970s, it is common to the field in general. So, for example, community based disposals for offenders have been evaluated without ever raising the issue as to whether their conclusions are equally applicable to males and females. Closer examination often reveals that either only males participated in the programme or, if females did so, gender differentials in outcome were either not inspected or not reported.

This project, therefore, provides an opportunity to write gender issues into our Review. It is partly an exercise in simple addition and subtraction; there are concerns generated by an examination of young female offenders which are additional to those already raised in our previous review, as well as issues raised in it which scarcely apply to young female offenders. But it could also be an exercise in reconstruction; some issues raised and developed by an examination of young female offenders compel some reconsideration of young males. This is perhaps the most exciting track to take, as well as being most deserving of its gender nomenclature.

In the area of aetiology, for example, the failure of criminologists to give women more than a footnote in works which purport to be on criminality in general has resulted in a lost opportunity, as much for the understanding of male criminality as female criminality (Morris 1987, Carlen 1988). Theories of male criminality, and particularly of young male criminality, are likely to have been quite different had young females and their relative absence from delinquent behaviour been taken into theoretical consideration. That they were not constitutes more than an interesting topic for the sociology of knowledge (Heidensohn 1985). It has also hindered the development of integrated theory, and has done little to provide for an informed body of knowledge to which policy makers and practitioners can refer. A similar objection might be raised against the vast research literature on the effectiveness of measures available to offenders. More conclusive statements as to "what works" might have been generated had some attention been paid, for example, to the lower rates of recidivism amongst female offenders.

The differences between the way in which males and females have been theoretically understood are even more striking when young offenders are considered. For young adult males, delinquency is generally conceived as a phase or 'stage' in life which young men are expected to grow out of unless some judicial or official intervention interferes with this seemingly natural process of maturation. Theories about female offenders, however, generally lack an age perspective. If male delinquency is frequently explained in terms of adolescence, "females are viewed as committing certain offences because of their sex rather than their age" (Gelsthorpe 1985). Shoplifting by young males, for example, is explained with reference to peer group pressure or the youthful search for excitement. At the same time, shoplifting by young females is explained in individualistic and pathological terms. Implicit in this perspective, then, is an assumption that whatever it is that explains the criminality of females, it is something to do with their femaleness. Nor will it therefore just go away with time. According to this understanding of female criminality, it must be addressed by some form of intervention if it is to change. While intervention in the lives of young males is thought by many to be counterproductive, it is seen to be a necessary, if not sufficient, requirement of rehabilitation for young females.

Raising the question as to why some people do not commit crimes rather than why some do, a few steps towards a theory with the ability to integrate male and female criminality have been made by Hirschi (1969). Hirschi proposed that social bonding - through attachment, involvement, commitment and belief - protected against participation in criminal activities. Though he did not include females in studies conducted to test his general theory, Hirschi's ideas have been taken up by the new feminist criminology (Heidensohn 1985, Morris 1987, Carlen 1988) to explain why criminal tendencies amongst women are inhibited.

In recent years, Braithwaite's (1989) steps towards an integrated theory have taken him somewhat further along the same path. In the first place, he has sought to construct a theory which will explain the relative strength of different groups as they appear in the criminal statistics, including males and females. Indeed, his theory of shame emphasises the critical importance to criminal theory of explaining the observed imbalance between the sexes in criminal activity. Secondly, he has attempted to deduce a successful penal strategy from his theory. Girls and women are inhibited from engaging in criminal activity because they are more disposed to feelings of shame and guilt. This is made possible because they are subject to greater degrees of informal social control (shame) and develop a stronger sense of self-control (guilt). Both reflect the greater involvement and dependency of females on others. This is because, in one form or another, girls and women are more bound to the community. Braithwaite suggests that for all offenders, therefore, measures which promote communal affiliation and social attachment are more likely to be effective in the prevention of recidivism than those which do not.

Some of these themes will be picked up again in the course of this report. For the most part, however, its aims are less ambitious - to address our omissions by raising those issues which are particular to female offenders. This report, then, is primarily an exercise in addition and not re-formulation.

Issues particular to female offenders arise because of the relative infrequency of their appearance in the criminal justice and related systems, because of assumptions and beliefs about gender which operate throughout society, and because of the particular social situation in which young women who offend are to be found. During the course of our previous work, the following issues concerning young adult female offenders emerged quite clearly from the literature reviewed:

1. Their very paucity may itself be problematic, leaving young adult female offenders liable to being treated as "doubly deviant". Females who offend are seen to be worse than their male counterparts -either very bad or very sick- even though their offences may be similar.

2. Young adult female offenders may therefore face greater risks of being escalated up the tariff system at a faster pace than young adult males, though they start off

on a "lower tariff". Hence, for example, there are a greater proportion of women on probation for minor transgressions and first offences than men. A repeat offence, even of a minor nature, is more likely to move women up the tariff to prison.

3. Girls and women may be more vulnerable to the process of net-widening than males. This may further aggravate the risk of their speedier movement up tariff.

4. The full range of disposals and measures may not be equally available to young adult female offenders. Beliefs about the nature of female offending and female offenders may be more crucial in determining how females are dealt with than any legal criteria, such as previous record or nature of offence.

5. The number of young adult female offenders in Scotland at present in prison under sentence or on remand is low, compared with young males. At the same time, it is higher than many industrialised counties in England, and it is far higher than most European countries. A larger proportion of females are in prison for petty property offences and, because they are less likely to re-offend, with no previous custodial sentence. Indeed, a significant minority of the female prison population of the U.K. have no previous conviction at all. Custody might have much to do with extra- legal criteria, such as homelessness and destitution.

6. Legislation of the past few years has spawned many new programmes and community based disposals, including those most recently designed to divert young people from criminal and disruptive behaviour. Yet they appear to have been developed without due consideration as to how young women may be included. This may have further contributed to the marginalisation of female offenders in the criminal justice system.

7. Because of the history and current situation of many young adult female offenders, community disposals -however promising the content of their programmes and however effective their implementation- may not be sufficient in themselves to prevent recidivism. Education, housing, employment and welfare provision may be crucial to back up even the best community based disposals.

8. At the same time, a few very successful projects and measures, some of which support women who are vulnerable to custodial sentence, have been established. Because they are dependent upon voluntary and short term support, or upon the commitment and the enthusiasm of one or two staff members, their existence is precarious, their continuity in doubt, and knowledge of them is fragmentary and localised.

Part 2, then, seeks to address issues which do not find exact parallels in our previous review. It will therefore proceed along somewhat different lines to include the following :

Literature Review: The central theme of our initial literature review was the effectiveness of measures and disposals available to young adult offenders. But as far as female young adult offenders are concerned, the question of "What Works" is noticeable by its absence from the literature. It is not the effectiveness of measures and disposals for female offenders that informs the literature. It is what measures and disposals are made available to women in the criminal justice system, and on what criteria those decisions are made. Issues generated by the question of differential sentencing and not the effectiveness of sentencing, then, provide this section with its organisational focus.

Young Offenders and Gender: The Scottish Evidence: Because the theme of this research exercise is somewhat different, it is possible to introduce and integrate statistical information already collected and available for Scotland into the report. This will be employed to assess and evaluate some of the issues raised by the literature review for their significance and relevance to the Scottish scene. This is done through an examination, albeit rudimentary, of the most recent published and unpublished Prison, Court and Community Service statistics for Scotland.

Successful Initiatives and Concluding Remarks: Recent measures to provide community based disposals as an alternative to custody for young female adults will be examined. Successful initiatives will be identified, and the testimony of participants in these initiatives will be discussed in an attempt to begin thinking critically about the criteria and ingredients of their success.

Chapter One

Gender and Differential Treatment in the Criminal Justice System : A Review of the Research Literature

In our initial report, Martinson's (1982) claim that "nothing works" provided a focus around which to review the literature. There is no comparable substantive material concerning young adult female offenders, nor even relating to female offenders in general. The question of what measures are most effective has scarcely been raised in relationship to females. Nor does there exist published debate over the appropriate criteria by which effectiveness should be measured. Instead, the central issue for debate has been whether or not female offenders are treated differently in the criminal justice system and, if so, how?

Grounds for the debate were laid by Pollak (1950) in what is considered to be the first major post war work on women and crime, *The Criminality of Women*. In it, Pollak sought to explain what he thought to be unreasonably low official female crime rates by invoking a protective disposition which, so he claimed, men display towards women;

> *"..men hate to accuse women...police officers dislike to arrest*
> *them, district attorneys to prosecute them, judges and juries*
> *to find them guilty"*.... (quoted in Klein, 1976).

According to Pollak, then, it is this general protective predisposition on the part of men - the chivalry factor - which accounts for the leniency with which he believed women to be treated in the male dominated criminal justice system.

If the research literature which followed in subsequent decades does not always refer to Pollak by name, what was produced may nevertheless be seen to represent a response to his theory of chivalry. Certainly, the major findings which emerge from this corpus of research provide a challenge to Pollak's position. They may usefully be pulled together and organised around the different arguments by which their challenge is constituted. At least four different strands of empirically supported argument can be discerned.

(i) Chivalry and Leniency

Published statistics confirm that women and girls are more likely to receive conditional discharges, probation orders, cautions and supervision orders, and less likely to receive custodial sentences, than males. On the face of it, then, it would seem that female offenders are treated more leniently than males in the criminal justice system. The chivalry hypothesis has been challenged, however, by breaking down aggregate sentencing statistics and analysing them by severity of offence and the past record of offenders. Disposals which appear lenient because of their position on the sentencing tariff may not appear to be so when offence and past record are taken into account. Much of what might appear to reflect leniency towards female offenders, then, may be accounted for by purely legal criteria and not by chivalry at all.

Perhaps the best U.K. example of this kind of work is Farrington and Morris's (1983) study of the Cambridge City Magistrates Court. As a proportion of all sentences, over twice as many men as women were found to have received severe sentences. Nevertheless, this was not sufficient to confirm the chivalry and leniency hypothesis. When sentences were controlled for offence and prior record, all differences between males and females disappeared and no evidence of greater leniency in the sentencing of females remained.

(ii) Chivalry, Gender and Separate Spheres

Statistical analyses, however, have allowed only a partial glimpse into the process of criminal court adjudication. Qualitative studies have been necessary to identify the methods by which sentencers justify the measures they dispense and, in the course of doing so, they have discovered chivalry to operate in some spheres but not in others. This cannot be accounted for by Pollak's theory.

Pollak saw his own work as a development of W.I. Thomas's *Sex and Society*, (1907). Yet in many ways it lacks much of Thomas's subtlety. Thomas had observed that women were not treated uniformly in all spheres of activity, but severely in some and leniently in others;

> " *man is merciless to woman from the standpoint of personal behaviour, yet he exempts her from anything in the way of contractual morality and views her defection in this regard with allowance and even amusement*" (quoted in Klein, 1976).

Thomas proposed that this could be explained by the different codes to which men and women were subject at that time. Because women occupied a marginal position in the productive sphere of exchange commodities, they also occupied a marginal position in regard to the law which regulates property and production. On the other hand, because they occupied a central place in the private sphere, they occupied a pivotal position in the codes which governed that sphere. Unlike Pollak, then, Thomas may be said to have produced a theory that is both historically and socially grounded. Different spheres of women's activities and behaviour are not responded to identically but are selected for severe or lenient treatment in a non-random and structured fashion, depending on the location in which women are situated in the social structure. Variations between spheres cannot be adequately explained, then, by the presence of some generalizable, innate and automatic chivalrous predisposition of men towards women.

Research findings give Thomas's theory strong support. In her observational study of a magistrates court, Worrall (1981) found the most decisive factor influencing the sentencing of male offenders to be their offences. For females offenders, however, the most decisive factors were demeanour in court and competence at home. Female offenders who were modest, humble and remorseful, and who successfully conformed to the domestic role, were considered to be "out of place" in the criminal justice system and were treated leniently. Those who did not conform to the conventional female role were treated far more harshly, (see also Gelsthorpe's (1985) study of a juvenile bureau, Worrall's (1990) examination of the discourse by which offending women are understood, and Hedderman's (1990) research on sentencing in a magistrates' court). Similarly, Carlen's (1983) study of Scottish sheriffs showed them unprepared to send female offenders to prison if they were judged to be competent mothers, or if their domestic arrangements were steady. In all of these studies, conformity to the domestic role and to the appropriate personality attributes which are expected to accompany it provide justification for decisions in the criminal justice system. Processing in the criminal justice system, then, can be understood, "as a way of patrolling and controlling the boundaries of the female role" (Morris 1987).

This also helps to explain why some offences are treated harshly in the criminal justice system, notwithstanding the good showing of female offenders in the domestic sphere. Where role expectations are breached in addition to the criminal law as, for example, in crimes of violence, then female offenders are likely to be more severely punished than men (Nagel 1981). This is also likely to be the case if women are convicted in the company of others (Farrington and Morris 1983). Since female criminal behaviour is assumed to be a private and not a social act, female offenders whose offences are perceived to be social/sociable in character are more severely punished than those whose are not. For young men and boys, then, peer pressure is to be expected and may have a mitigating effect on their sentencing. For females, deviance in groups is doubly deviant.

(iii) Chivalry and the Differentiation of Women

Just as the different spheres within which women move may be differentially subject to chivalrous behaviour, so may different women. Pollak's theory has been attacked as sexist, racist and classist in that it invokes a sweeping claim for what men feel and behave towards all women, irrespective of race or class. It may be challenged, therefore, by closer scrutiny of the treatment and sentencing of different social categories of females in the criminal justice system.

This has been undertaken in relation to class and race and, more recently, in relation to marital status. It is questionable, for example, as to whether police deal more leniently with women in general. What the data seem to show is that leniency is reserved for the passive, unaggressive, remorseful white middle class woman (Morris 1987). Certainly there is much current concern in the U.K. over the apparent severity with which black women are dealt with in the criminal justice system, particularly in relation to custodial sentencing, (NACRO, 1989; Genders and Players 1989; National Youth Agency 1992). At the time of their recent inspection of the female prison population, HM Inspectorate of Probation (1991) found 25% of all female prisoners to be from ethnic minorities, only one third of whom could be accounted for by drug trafficking.

In the course of this research, no U.K. findings with bearing on the relationship of class to the operation of chivalry in the criminal justice system were found. The absence of data may reflect one of several things: the small number of middle class girls and women who come before the courts, the difficulty which social scientists have in dealing with class or socio-economic status in relation to females, as well as what social researchers may have taken for granted. Marital status, on the other hand, has been the subject of much discussion. While marital status appears to have no significant effect on the sentencing of male offenders, it is a decisive factor in the sentencing of female offenders, both in the U.K. and the U.S.(Nagel 1981). In Farrington and Morris's (1983) Cambridge study, for example, divorced and separated women were more likely to receive severe sentences than married women, whereas marital status had no independent effect on the sentencing of male offenders. Bail decisions were also found to work in favour of married women (Eaton 1983).

Chivalry thus extends only as far as those women for whom men feel protective towards, and no further. Paternalism is particularistic, unpredictable and non-rational. The stuff of chivalry, therefore, is contrary to everything which the rule of law stands for, namely, universalism, predictability and rationality.

(iv) Chivalry as Oppression

Pollak's theory may be challenged by further examination of the protectiveness which underlies the spirit of chivalry, and by scrutinization of its consequences for female offenders. Focusing on chivalry, and not on the protectiveness and paternalism in which it is embedded, diverts attention both from the power relationships which accompany chivalrous behaviour, and from the consequences of the exercise of that power. If chivalry is based on a desire to protect and support, then it rests upon the belief that some people have special qualities such that they require more protection and support than others. In the criminal justice system, women - like children - are believed to be less aware and less responsible for their actions (Pearson 1976) and thus deserving of special protection. The nature of chivalry is Janus-faced, however, for while paternalism may foster leniency, it may easily lead with much good intention down the path to greater oppression. In the criminal justice system, this takes the form of "net -widening" and tariff escalation.

(a) Protection, Welfare and Net-widening

The potential of chivalry for oppression in the criminal justice system may be found in its tendency towards net-widening. It has been identified particularly in relation to children and women, and therefore makes a double impact upon girls and young women.

Net-widening occurs when particular welfare needs are perceived to exist which, though not justified by legal criteria, are dealt with or managed through the criminal justice system. The encouragement of non-delinquent girls to join Intermediate Treatment groups exemplifies the process of gender-related netwidening. In his major review of Intermediate Treatment in England and Wales, Bottoms (1990) found just 20% of all participants to be girls. But whereas 80% of all boys participating in the programmes were offenders, only 25% of the girls were. The net widening effect of Intermediate Treatment for girls, so his review suggests, is a major cause for concern.

Cautioning is subject to similar suspicion. It has been used in England and Wales as a diversion from court mainly in response to offences committed by children and young adults, and particularly girls and young adult females. At first glance, this may appear to reflect greater leniency towards females and children, or at least be explained away by their lesser offences or records. However, there is strong and ample evidence to suggest that the higher proportion of young people and females cautioned may not reflect leniency at all (Farrington and Bennett 1981, NACRO 1990). Indeed, all the empirical evidence points to the contrary. Cautions are now being given for conduct which hitherto brought no further action, and the use of cautioning in England and Wales is bringing large numbers of non-delinquent girls into the juvenile justice system who might otherwise not be there.

Similar findings emerge from examination of diversionary programmes set up for adults, for example, in the Scottish diversion to social work schemes (Stedward and Millar 1989). In the sample of diversion referrals selected for study, women constituted 44% of all referrals. This is in marked contrast to 12% of all those who were prosecuted against in 1986, the year of study. Again, the higher than expected proportion of females diverted was found not to reflect greater leniency, but rather the opposite. Because diversion was motivated by welfare considerations and not legal criteria, many women for whom prosecution would have been deemed inappropriate were now falling into the criminal justice system.

The protective nature of chivalry also explains why profound differences exist between boys and girls in the offences for which they are brought before the court, as well as in their disposals. Girls are far more likely to come before the court for status offences and moral danger than boys. Thus, over half the girls appearing in a London juvenile court over a three month period were found to be brought to court for non-criminal matters. While the majority of girls were given care or supervision orders, the boys were mainly fined (Casburn 1979). Similarly, in another of the few studies comparing male and female juvenile offenders before the courts, magistrates were found to be taking a far more interventionist approach towards girls than boys - supervision and care orders were the disposals they most favoured for the girls, and fines or discharge for the boys (Parker et al. 1981).

In a further study of juveniles subject to supervision orders, girls were found to have committed less serious offences than boys, been involved in fewer current offences and had fewer past convictions (Webb 1984). From an analysis of their files, Webb found girls to be presumed suitable for supervision without specification of the particular needs which social work might be called in to address. For girls, rule breaking *per se* is problematic - it constitutes incontrovertible evidence of the presence of a problem. Thus, as Webb concludes, criminal proceedings give ample scope for welfare interventions far beyond the demand of justice alone. While all young offenders may be sentenced on the basis of welfare considerations, the discretion which this allows has the effect of leaving girls subject to a greater distortion of the principle of proportionality than boys. This point is strongly exemplified in a study of a secure assessment facility made over the course of one year. Only one quarter of the girls were found to be brought there because of their delinquent behaviour. The most frequent initial cause was 'absconding', and the main reason given for placement was "protection" (Morris and Wilkinson 1983).

(b) Protection and Tariff Escalation

Women reach the top of the sentencing tariff by virtue of having committed several minor transgressions rather than any major ones (Jackson and Smith 1987). Indicative of the seriousness of the offences for which women are imprisoned is the length of their term of sentence. Of the 2,650 women received into custody under sentence of immediate imprisonment in England and Wales in 1989, 69% were sentenced for 12 months and under. An inspection of six Prison Service establishments holding 80% of the female prison population in England and Wales in 1989 examined Social Inquiry Reports which are made for all persons who are in danger of receiving a custodial sentence either for the first time or because they are under 21. It found that 57% of all women for whom Social Inquiry Reports were available were in prison for petty theft, small scale fraud and the possession of drugs for personal use, that is, for offences which themselves demanded community disposals. Why these women should be serving a prison sentence was raised as a question of the highest urgency by HM Inspectorate of Probation (1991).

The unjustified escalation of female offenders to the top of the sentencing tariff may be accounted for, paradoxically, by the welfare model of probation which both probation officers and sentencers employ with regard to female offenders. Probation's position as the most favoured disposal in the sentencing tariff for women is not based on legal criteria. Since welfare considerations predominate, female offenders very often receive probation where, for similar offences, male offenders receive fines. This makes ex-probationers more vulnerable to a custodial sentence should they re-appear before the courts for offending behaviour.

Partly, then, women graduate onto the medium to high rungs of the tariff ladder far too quickly. This does not fully explain why they do not stay there, however, rather than escalating to the top of the ladder and custody. Some clue is provided by the Probation Inspectorate's examination of Social Inquiry Reports for women held in custody on non-serious offences. Almost without exception, their principal recommendation to the bench had been either probation or a suspended prison sentence - which, needless to say, had been rejected in favour of custody. Why, so the report asks, had so many Social Inquiry reports not raised the possibility of Community Service? Or why had the option of a probation order with Schedule 11/4A or 4B (day centre and intensive probation) requirements not been brought to the attention of the court so as to provide further options of community based disposals?

As far as Community Service is concerned, research findings do help us begin to answer these questions. Jackson and Smith (1987) found that for the majority of their prison sample of female offenders, Community Service had not been seriously considered in Social Inquiry Reports because of domestic circumstances. The Probation Inspectorate (1991) found much the same in its analysis of Social Inquiry Reports. Community Service had been assessed as a non-viable option either because of motherhood responsibilities or because of low self confidence which, so it was feared, would only be exacerbated by Community Service. Similarly, Carlen (1990) found a prejudice amongst probation officers against Community Service for women because of the lack of creche facilities- whether real or imagined. Interestingly, only a few probation officers were suspected of not recommending Community Service for female offenders because of the absence of appropriate 'woman's work'. These findings suggest, then, that it is concern for the welfare of female offenders, and particularly concern for how they will manage their domestic / mothering responsibilities that prevents probation officers from recommending Community Service. The cruel irony is that their hesitation may have disastrous consequences for the welfare of female offenders and their children.

Yet this can only provide a partial explanation. The absence of creches are often more imagined than real, and not all female offenders passed over by probation officers and sentencers for Community Service have responsibility for children. We might begin to understand the hesitation with which Community Service is recommended for females if we go on to consider why so many female offenders in custody have not been considered for probation with Schedule 11/4A or 4B (day centre and intensive probation) requirements. This is a particularly important issue to raise because, for the many reasons which we have documented in our initial report, these disposals have become the most promising measures available for keeping in the community those offenders, and particularly young adult offenders, who might otherwise have been imprisoned. Yet, as the Probation Inspectorate found, it is a measure rarely considered for female offenders in England and Wales. This is perhaps because, like Community Service, probation with a schedule 11/4A or 4B requirement is perceived to function as punishment in the community rather than as a method by which to help promote the welfare of offenders. Both disposals are measures which are commonly understood to orient to the offences and actions of offenders, who are thereby considered to be in control and responsible for their actions (McWilliams 1981). As such, they do not fit with the conventional view of female offenders which finds them needy, not fully responsible for their actions, and requiring, above all else, special protection and support. The welfare model, to which female offenders are so much more susceptible, sits uneasily with those community based disposals currently providing the best opportunity for avoiding custody and remaining in the community. As long as the welfare model predominates, then, female offenders will be in prison for offences which do not justify incarceration.

Chapter Two

Young Offenders and Gender: The Scottish Evidence

This chapter is devoted to examining the available Scottish statistical data for replication of findings reported in previous sections. It begins with some background data to the study by examining changes in the rates and patterns of offending in Scotland by gender. Some consideration is also given to the relationship between age, gender and offending behaviour. The primary objective of this chapter, however, is to establish whether there is support for the hypotheses generated by our discussion of chivalry. The range of hypotheses which may be examined at present is limited by the availability of pre-existing data. Their analysis may indicate the value of pursuing this line of inquiry further. Without more sophisticated statistical techniques and empirical research, however, it cannot be stressed strongly enough that any claims made on the basis of these data to support or reject the hypotheses remain tentative.

(i) Gender and Crime in Scotland

Charges on all crimes and offences were proved against 168,382 persons in Scotland in 1991, of whom only 15% were female. This represents a decrease in the number and proportion of males convicted between 1987 and 1991, and marks an increase in the number and proportion of females convicted over the same years.

	Number			Per cent	
All crimes and offences	**Male**	**Female**	**All**	**Males**	**Female**
1988	152,527	22,472	176,046	87	13
1989	147,545	23,006	171,163	86	13
1990	149,545	24,194	173,924	86	14
1991	142,788	25,484	168,383	85	15

Persons with charge proved.

When only crimes are examined, however, a somewhat different picture emerges:

Number				**Per cent**	
All crimes	**Male**	**Female**	**All**	**Males**	**Female**
1988	48,821	7554	56,805	86	13
1989	45,928	7211	53,320	86	14
1990	45,638	7686	53,399	85	14
1991	42,364	7149	49,564	85	14

Persons with charge proved.

The reduction in crimes and offences over the four year period is mainly due to a fall in the number of persons with crimes proved against them. Though the proportion of females with charges proved against them increases very slightly over these years, their actual numbers decrease. They do not decrease, however, at the same rate as males. As far as types of crimes are concerned, there are slight increases in the number and proportion of females convicted of serious assault, handling offensive weapons and robbery. There is also a substantial increase over these years in the numbers of women convicted of crimes of indecency under the category of "other" (prostitution offences), and in the number and proportion of females convicted of fraud. There is only a slight increase in the number and proportion of females convicted of shoplifting, however, and quite a considerable decrease in the number and proportion of females convicted of "other theft".

Between 1988 and 1991, there was a very slight fall in the number of persons convicted of offences which was mainly the responsibility of males. Females, on the other hand, show a large increase in actual numbers, as well as making an increasing contribution to the total.

	Number			Per cent	
All Offences	**Male**	**Female**	**All**	**Males**	**Female**
1988	103,706	14,918	119,241	87	13
1989	101,732	15,795	117,843	86	13
1990	103,907	16,508	120,525	86	14
1991	100,424	18,335	118,818	85	15

Persons with charge proved.

Two thirds of this increase, however, is represented by motor vehicle offences-partially by reckless and careless driving as well as unlawful use of vehicle, but more particularly by speeding offences which showed a considerable and steady increase amongst females over the years. Nevertheless, females convicted of motoring offences in 1991 still comprised only 10% of all persons convicted on these offences. Nearly one third of the increase in females convicted on offences is for 'other' miscellaneous offences (under which non - payment for TV licences is included). It would be rash to interpret these increases, therefore, as indicative of a general trend towards females "becoming more like males". Indeed, poverty and rising numbers of single parents families may be responsible for the increase in females convicted of 'other' miscellaneous offences. The increase in "speeding" amongst women, however, is quite intriguing.

In 1991, and with an overall average proportion of 15%, females contributed more than 10% to the number of persons convicted for the following crimes and offences in Scotland:

	% Females
'Other' non-sexual crimes of violence (mainly against children)	56
'Other 'crimes of indecency (mainly prostitution related)	74
Shoplifting	33
'Other' theft	16
Fraud	26
'Other' crimes of dishonesty (mainly embezzlement, forgery)	14
Fire-raising	15
Crimes against public justice	11
Simple assault	11
'Other' miscellaneous offences (mainly parking, TV licence)	48

(ii) Age, Gender and Crime

Commonly held assumptions of female delinquency lack the age perspective of male delinquency. Males, unlike females, are believed to offend because of their age and unlike female offenders, their offending behaviour will decrease with age. Whether or not this assumption finds support in the Scottish statistics may be examined by inspecting the rates of charges proved against males and females of different age groups.

Rate per 10,000 population

Age	Males	Females
15	27	2
16	530	62
17	972	127
18	1,055	124
19	1,042	113
20	926	107
25	553	88
30	368	69
35	249	52
40	193	37
45	161	29

Individuals with at least one charge proved for crimes groups 1 to 5, simple assault and breach of the peace, Scotland 1990.

Measured by charges proved, these figures indicate that females exhibit much the same pattern as males. If charges proved against females peak at ages 17 and 18 to 127 / 124 per 10,000, they peak slightly later for males at ages 18 and 19 to 1,055 / 1,042 per 10,000. By age 25, the rate for females has fallen to 88 per 10,000 and slightly more rapidly for males to 553 per 10,000. By age 30, the rate has fallen to half of what it was at its peak for females and to a third of what it was at its peak for males. For both males and females, the rate of conviction per 10,000 halves again between ages 30 to 40, so that by age 40 it is 29% of what it was at its peak for females, and 18% for males. Thus, the rate of conviction for Scottish females shows a substantial decline between ages 16 and 40, though not quite as dramatic a decline as for males.

The pattern which emerges from these data provides quite convincing evidence that for females, as with males, crime is very much a youth related phenomenon in Scotland. However, the disparity between males and females in the actual numbers of convictions is very large. In 1990, charges were proved against 39,546 males and against 3,843 females between the ages of 16 and 20. This great gender difference in actual numbers of convictions is possibly responsible for overlooking the age related pattern of offending behaviour amongst females. To overlook and ignore this pattern, however, helps sustain the myth of female criminality as individualistic, pathological and essentially non-social.

(iii) Gender, Chivalry and Leniency

Females, so Pollak proposes, are treated more leniently at all levels of the criminal justice system. Recent research suggests, however, that when aggregate data are broken down by offence and past record, any tendency of the criminal justice system towards leniency for females disappears.

Initial police reports on children for all ages in Scotland do suggest some evidence of greater leniency for girls. Of all children against whom some police action was taken, the following **percentages** of girls and boys were warned, referred to the Reporter, or to the Procurator Fiscal in 1989:

All Actions	Warning	Reporter	Procurator Fiscal
Boys (100%)	10.1	77.1	12.8
Girls (100%)	19.4	68.9	11.6

Initial police reports on children for all ages in Scotland, 1989.

Thus, girls were almost twice as likely to receive a warning than boys. However, for the severest action which might be taken by the police, namely, referral to the Procurator Fiscal, gender differences appear to be insignificant..

This pattern is repeated for boys and girls aged 15:

All Actions	Warning	Reporter	Procurator Fiscal
Boys (100%)	5.4	73.5	21.1
Girls (100%)	14.3	67.4	18.3

Initial police reports on children aged 15 in Scotland, 1989.

At age 15, then, both boys and girls are less likely to receive a warning than children of all ages. 15 year old girls, however, are almost three times as likely to receive a warning as boys. Nevertheless, they are only slightly less likely to be referred to the Procurator Fiscal. Evidence of leniency on aggregate exists, then, but only at the lower end of the tariff.

This may be accounted for by legal criteria, such as past record or type of offending behaviour, rather than chivalry on the part of police. Data are available which make possible control for type of offence, but not for record. Of the 1,087 15 year old girls on whom police filed reports in Scotland in 1989, 75% of all offences were for Shoplifting (N= 249), Petty Assault (N= 237), Breach of the Peace (N= 189) and Other Theft (N= 93). Comparing boys with girls for police response to their offending behaviour, girls were almost twice as likely to receive a warning than boys on each of these offences. At the same time, they were almost as likely as boys to be referred to the Procurator Fiscal on each of these offences.

All Actions	Warning	Procurator Fiscal
Shoplifting		
Boys (100%)	11.8	17.2
Girls(100%)	20.1	15.7
Petty Assault		
Boys(100%)	5.5	16.9
Girls(100%)	10.5	14.3
Breach of the Peace		
Boys(100%)	6.0	17.3
Girls(100%)	11.6	16.4
Other Theft		
Boys(100%)	5.0	16.8
Girls(100%)	9.7	16.1

Initial police reports on boys and girls, aged 15 , by offence, in Scotland 1989.

What these data indicate, then, is that for offences in which 15 years old girls are most likely to participate, they are still twice as likely to be given warnings than boys. At the same time, girls are almost as likely as boys to be referred to the Procurator Fiscal. The patterns, therefore, reflect the aggregate data. Gender differentials in the actions police take cannot be explained away different types of offences they commit, though there may be differences between boys and girls in the gravity of their behaviour within an offence type. Overall, girls are treated slightly more leniently. The very minimal differences in the proportion of boys and girls referred to the Procurator Fiscal on aggregate and for each of the offences examined should be particularly noted, however, and requires some explanation. It would appear that chivalry is operating for girls at one end of the tariff, but not at the other. This may partly, if not fully, be explained by the lack of discretion allowed to the police as to who they are obliged to refer on to the Procurator Fiscal. In the case of offences which lie higher up the tariff system, the police are given less discretionary powers and, thus, less opportunity for the display of chivalry.

The sentencing structure of young adults may be subjected to a similar analysis:

All Penalties	Per cent				
	Other	Fine	Probation	CSO	Custody
Males (100%)	13.0	67.1	4.3	5.6	10.1
Females (100%)	24.9	61.0	7.7	2.2	4.2

Young Adults (16-20 years old) with charges proved in Scotland 1990.

Young adult males in Scotland in 1990 were more than twice as likely as females to be sentenced to custody and half as likely to be given sentences categorised as "Other", that is, absolute discharge, caution or admonition. Males were almost three times as likely to receive Community Service, while females were almost twice as likely to receive probation, and slightly less likely to be given a fine. In terms of both ends of the sentencing tariff, therefore, young adult females were clearly treated more leniently on aggregate. The middle ranges are more problematic, since the position of 'middle range' penalties on the leniency- severity continuum are more difficult to locate.

The picture changes little when the nature of female offending behaviour is taken into consideration and sentencing is controlled for type of offence. In 1990, 53% of all charges (N=3843) against young adult females were accounted for by breach of the peace (N=435), shoplifting (N=532), other theft (N=432), petty assault (N=405), and crimes against public justice (N=210).

All Penalties	Per cent				
	Other	Fine	Probation	CSO	Custody
Shoplifting					
Males (100%)	16.6	58.8	7.3	3.5	13.8
Female (100%)	24.8	54.3	11.1	2.8	7.0
Other Theft					
Males (100%)	14.4	47.5	8.8	10.7	8.6
Females (100%)	32.4	46.8	10.2	3.0	7.6
Crimes vs. Public Justice					
Males (100%)	18.5	51.3	5.8	6.8	17.6
Females (100%)	31.4	44.3	10.0	4.3	10.0
Petty Assault					
Males (100%)	13.7	66.0	4.3	7.1	9.0
Females (100%)	35.6	51.1	7.4	2.7	3.2
Breach of Peace					
Males (100%)	17.5	77.8	1.3	1.3	2.1
Females (100%)	34.3	60.2	3.9	0.5	1.1

Males and females aged 16 to 20 with charges proved in Scotland 1990.

When broken down by type of offence, differential sentencing rates faithfully reflect the pattern of aggregate sentencing. For offences usually at the lower end of the sentencing tariff, young adult males are two to three times more likely to receive Community Service and custody, and slightly more likely to receive fines, than females. Young adult females, on the other hand, are more likely to receive probation and twice as likely to receive an admonition or absolute discharge. Thus, those offences for which young adult females are most likely to be convicted do not account for and explain away the gender differentials found in the aggregate sentencing data.

If gender differentials in sentencing cannot be accounted for by the different offences on which young adult males and females are convicted, then it is possible that their criminal records can. There are data available on the number of convictions any individual receives in a single year, though not on their full criminal record. The analysis therefore remains tentative. If we examine penalties imposed on 16 to 20 year olds (Scotland) convicted only once in a single year, (1990), however, the same pattern is evident. Females are twice as likely as males to receive an admonition or absolute discharge and more than twice as likely to receive probation. At the same time, males are somewhat more likely to receive a fine, more than twice as likely to receive a Community Service Order and almost four times as likely to be given a custodial sentence.

	Per cent				
All Penalties	**Other**	**Fine**	**Probation**	**CSO**	**Custody**
Males (N=11,050)	19.3	70.3	2.7	4.2	3.3
Females (N=1,440)	35.0	56.7	5.7	1.7	0.9

Penalties associated with a single conviction amongst 16-20 year olds in 1990.

The greater leniency displayed towards young adult females might be explained away when types of offences on which they have been convicted are also taken into account.

The data do not show this to be the case. On four of the six offences on which young adult females tend to be most often convicted, they are twice as likely to receive admonitions and absolute discharges than males, and on the other two, (Shoplifting and Crimes vs. Public Justice), they are still more likely to do so though considerably less so than for the other offences. Except for the curious reversal in Crimes vs. Public Justice, young adult females are always more likely to receive probation than males, and males are very much more likely than females to receive a Community Service Order or a custodial sentence. The patterns of sentencing therefore appear to shadow the aggregate data. Controlling for type of offence does not make the gender differential disappear.

There still remains the possibility that more sophisticated statistical techniques and case information might be able to explain the greater leniency with which young adult females are sentenced in Scotland in non-chivalrous, legal terms. As it stands,

All Penalties	Per cent				
	Other	Fine	Probation	CSO	Custody
Shoplifting					
Males (N= 285)	24.6	71.2	1.4	1.8	1.0
Females(N= 208)	31.7	63.5	4.8	0.0	0.0
Other Theft					
Males(N=1,036)	20.3	70.0	4.0	3.6	2.5
Females(N=243)	40.0	51.4	5.8	2.0	1.2
Crimes v Public Justice					
Males(N=471)	20.6	68.2	1.9	3.8	5.5
Females(N=85)	29.4	60.0	1.6	7.1	2.4
Petty Assault					
Males(N=1,632)	18.0	71.9	2.8	4.9	2.5
Females(N=248	40.3	56.0	2.4	0.4	0.4
Breach of Peace					
Males(N=3,021)	20.8	77.1	0.7	0.9	0.5
Females(1N-255)	35.7	63.5	0.8	0.0	0.0
Fraud					
Males (N=161)	11.8	83.2	1.9	2.5	0.6
Females(N=91)	23.0	68.1	0.5	0.3	0.0

Penalties associated with a single conviction amongst 16-20 year olds in Scotland, 1990, by offences for which young adult females are most commonly convicted.

however, the Scottish data on young offenders do not appear to replicate Farrington and Morris's (1983) study of a Cambridge Magistrates Court. When sentencing is controlled for type of offence and partially controlled for record, evidence of greater leniency in the sentencing of young adult females remains.

(iv) Gender, Chivalry and Separate Spheres

It has been suggested that the severity or leniency with which females are sentenced depend upon the extent to which they are perceived to conform to traditional expectations. According to this hypothesis, offences which are not "true to type" will elicit the severest penalties.

From the available statistical data, types of offences may be arranged into a rank order according to degree of severity of action which they elicit. For example, the offences for which police action is taken against 15 year old girls may be ranked according to which are most likely to be referred by the police to the Procurator Fiscal. This may then be compared with actions taken against 15 year olds boys for similar offences:

Referral to the Procurator Fiscal

	Number		Per cent	
	Girls	Boys	Girls	Boys
1. Other Motor Vehicle	3	19	75	41
2. Robbery	2	25	67	36
3. Serious Assault	8	62	67	44
4. Unlawful Use of Vehicle	2	77	67	66
5. Theft-Motor Vehicle	10	259	53	48
6. Theft OLP	4	103	50	17
7. Drugs	2	13	50	25

Initial police action against 15 year olds in 1989 - numbers and percentages of all boys and all girls referred to the Procurator Fiscal for seven offences.

There are seven offences for which police take action against 50% or more girls by referring them to the Procurator Fiscal. Most significantly, boys are treated more leniently for all of these offences, and very much more leniently for five of them. For the six highest ranked offences, at least, it seems clear that behaviour is involved which runs contrary to traditional role expectations. The actual number of girls involved in these offences, of course, is quite small. There were only 8 cases of police action against 15 year old girls on serious assault and only 2 cases for robbery. Though the numbers involved are too small to warrant a confident analysis, this work may be taken further by aggregating numbers over several years. All that may be said with some certainly now is that girls charged with these offences appear to be triply deviant - not only with regard to the law and traditional gendered roles, but also because of their actual numbers. Rather than discounting them because of the size of their group, however, the likelihood of severe action being taken against them on non-legal criteria must be brought to general awareness.

The same kind of analysis may be undertaken for the 16-20 year age group, this time using custody, Community Service Orders and probation as indicators of profound action. The offences for which 16 to 20 year olds females are most likely to receive one of these three penalties are, as follows:

Custody, CSO or Probation

	Number		Per cent	
	Females	Males	Females	Males
1. Robbery	6	91	60	69
2. Other violence	4	6	57	46
3. Housebreaking	24	608	41	43
4. Assault	4	132	33	50

16 to 20 year old males and females receiving Custody, CSO or Probation 1990, by the four highest ranking offences for females.

These data show that for "robbery" and "housebreaking", that is, for what are conventionally male crimes, young adult females are dealt with almost as severely as males. It would be interesting to go on and compare males and females for the gravity of their offence to see if females are receiving penalties higher up the tariff for similar offences, that is, to see if they are being penalised for being "not true to type". What is significant is that young adult females are treated more severely for offences under the category of "other violence" (which covers "cruel and unnatural violence to children"), than for offences under "assault". As hypothesized earlier, chivalry does not appear to extend to that sphere within which females hold a pivotal position, namely, the domestic sphere.

Because sentencers treat probation as if it were lower down the tariff when they deal with females, it might be argued that the severity of penalty demonstrated above against young women is exaggerated. If custody alone is taken to be indicative of severity, then the likelihood of females receiving harsher penalties than males appears to be diminished. However, offences which rank highest for the severity of penalties which they elicit against female offenders remain most definitely outside what is traditionally female.

	Custody			
	Number		Per cent	
	Females	Males	Females	Males
1. Robbery	3	65	30	50
2 Crimes vs. Public Justice	9	115	7	13
3. Shoplifting	13	44	4	8
4. Housebreaking	2	259	3	19

16-20 year old males and females receiving Custody, 1990, by the four offences with highest ranking of custody for females.

At first appearance, then, young adult females do not seem to be receiving custodial sentences for offences at the same rate as males, even for offences which appear to be run contrary to conventional gender roles. On the other hand, the statistical sources available give little indication as to the seriousness of the offences within the offence type for which females and males are given custodial sentences. This, again, requires further investigation.

(v) Chivalry and the Differentiation of Women

It has been suggested that chivalry may extend only to certain categories of women - race, class and marital status being categories around which the chivalry of sentencers may vary. Neither *Criminal Proceedings in Scottish Courts* nor *Prison Statistics Scotland* provide information on these variables. Some apposite data, however, may be found in *The Community Service Bulletin 1992* for information on community service places given in 1990.

	Number		Per cent	
	Female	Male	Female	Male
Single	135	2,764	45.3	68.7
Married	98	1,008	32.9	25.0
Widowed, divorced and separated.	65	248	21.8	6.0
Total	298	4,020	100	100

Female and male offenders given Community Service in Scotland, by marital status, 1990.

Over two thirds of all males on Community Service in 1990 were single compared to less than 50% of all females. At the same time, over 30% of all females were married and 55% had been married at some, compared with only 31 per cent of all males. The higher proportion of married or once married females on Community Service cannot be explained away by any tendency for Community Service to be given to younger people. The figures do not simply reflect the fact that females marry earlier. Females referred to Community Service, and females given Community Service, tend to be considerably older than males, as the following numbers indicate:

	Number		Per cent	
Age	Female	Male	Female	Male
16-17	23	668	8	17
18-20	45	1,253	15	31
21-25	74	963	25	24
26-30	69	508	23	13
31-40	65	434	22	11
41+	24	218	8	8
Total	300	4,038	100	100

Numbers of offenders given Community Service in Scotland, by age and sex, 1990.

It is a matter of conjecture at this point why, compared to males, older married females are preferred over younger single females for Community Service in Scotland. Are older females preferred because they tend to be married, or are married females preferred because they tend to be older? Are older, married women more likely to be held responsible for their actions, and therefore perceived to be more appropriate Community Service placements? Or are they perceived to be less in need of restraint? What is certain, however, is that if younger, single females are not being referred to Community Service, their risk of receiving a custodial sentence is increased. Indeed, in 1988, when statistical information on sentencing was broken down by sex and narrow age bands, 16-17 year old female offenders were almost five times as likely to receive a custodial sentence (N=63) as Community Service in Scotland, while males of the same age were just over twice as likely (*Community Service Bulletin*

1990). The proportion of very young adult females receiving a custodial sentence rather than a high tariff community disposal in the years since 1988 seems a matter for closer examination and urgent review.

(vi) Chivalry as Oppression

(a) Protection, Welfare and Netwidening.

Whether and to what extent chivalry is responsible for netwidening is difficult to ascertain from an examination of the available statistical sources. In the case of children, we have already cited data to show that police in Scotland are more likely to issue warnings to girls than boys, even when the category of offence is held constant. Like police cautions in England and Wales, it could be that girls in Scotland are being given warnings for conduct which would bring no further action against boys. If it were possible to take gravity of offence into account, what might appear to be greater leniency towards girls may turn out to be netwidening. On the other hand, it might also be that girls are given unrecorded warnings for behaviour where boys are receiving formal warnings. Without further information, either interpretation is possible - girls receiving official warnings could be a different population from boys receiving official warnings, but we cannot say for certain what that difference is without further investigation.

Similarly, we noted that in Scotland (1990) young women aged 16 to 20 were almost twice as likely as males to receive an absolute discharge, caution or admonition for those offences for which charges against young adult females were most commonly proved. If gravity of offence could be taken into account, however, what apparently indicates greater leniency towards young female offenders may also turn out to be indicative of netwidening. Since young females are perceived to be more responsive to authority, netwidening might be operating not simply in the name of protection or welfare. Warnings, cautions and admonitions may be employed by and within the criminal justice system in pursuit of prevention and education in circumstances where, for males, no further action is deemed appropriate. There is a strong suspicion that a similar argument might explain the high proportion of young women who are remanded in custody but go on to receive a relatively minor penalty (Casale 1989). On the other hand, it may be that when gravity of offence is taken into account, young adult males receiving an absolute discharge or admonition are more like females who are never prosecuted in the first place. Again, it is not possible to develop this without further information.

Given the range of findings which support the existence of a strong tendency towards netwidening for females in England and Wales at various points in the criminal justice system, the apparent leniency with which statistical sources show young female offenders to be treated in Scotland at least requires further investigation.

(b) Protection, Probation and Tariff Escalation.

Probation occupies a favoured position in the sentencing tariff for females, and concern was raised in the literature review over the extra-legal, welfare oriented grounds on which its popularity rests. Of the 3,843 occasions on which a charge was proved against 16-20 year old females in Scotland (1990), 7.7% received probation orders compared to just 4.3% of all 39,546 occasions on which a crime was proved against 16-20 year old males. At the same time, fines were given for 61% of the crimes for which young adult females were convicted, as against 67% for males. This pattern remains when males and females are compared by offence, though it remains more strongly for some offences than others. For 16-20 year olds convicted of housebreaking, shoplifting, fraud and 'other dishonesty', females are more than twice as likely as males to receive probation orders.

It would be rash to conclude, however, that females receive probation where males receive fines. Since 16-20 year old males are more likely to receive custody (10% compared to 4% for females) and Community Service (5.6% compared to 2.2% for females), then it is at least possible that females are receiving probation orders where males are receiving sentences higher up the tariff. Since females are more likely to be admonished and discharged, then it is possible that this is occurring where males are receiving fines. Whether or not young adult females are escalated up-tariff to probation out of welfare considerations, therefore, remains uncertain. Like the issue of netwidening, available statistical sources are unlikely to provide the answer.

It has been suggested that welfare considerations lead to the up-tariffing of female offenders in a more indirect way. In a previous section, we noted the suggestion made by the Probation Inspectorate (1991) that female incarceration often results from the failure of Social Inquiry Reports requesting probation, and from the failure to promote more viable community disposals for female offenders. For 16-17 year old females against whom a charge was proved in Scotland in 1988, for example, 5% (63) were given a custodial sentence while only 1% (14) received a Community Service Order. In comparison, 16-17 year old males were only twice as likely to receive a custodial sentence as Community Service. The same information has not, unfortunately, been published in later statistical bulletins. Why such a high proportion of very young adult female offenders received custodial sentences requires further consideration.

It has been claimed (personal communication) that a high proportion of young female offenders are drug users, though the offences for which they are convicted are often minor and only indirectly drug-related. In such cases, either Community Service Orders would never have been entertained in the first place, or custodial sentences are given for relatively minor offences in the belief that offenders will be removed to a drug-free environment both for their own protection and rehabilitation.

It is doubtful, however, that the entire young adult female prison population in Scotland can be understood in terms of drug related offences. Even if it could, the appropriateness of custodial sentence would remain questionable. In 1990, 79 women under the age of 21 were received into prison under direct sentence. The paths which led them there can only be a matter of conjecture at this point.

Nevertheless, there appear to be gender inequities in the way in which Community Service Orders, as crucial and viable alternatives to custody, are given. Like males, 16-20 year old female offenders were twice as likely to be given a custodial sentence over a Community Service Order in Scotland in 1990. For some offences, however, the likelihood of females receiving a Community Service Order is equal, almost equal, or greater than their likelihood of receiving custody. These include housebreaking, handling weapons, theft (motor vehicles), fraud and other dishonesty, malicious and reckless conduct, and drugs.

	Custody		Community Service	
	Number	Per cent	Number	Per cent
Petty Assault	13	3	11	3
Drugs	2	3	2	3
Fraud	2	2	5	4
Other dishonesty	5	5	8	8
Theft Mot Veh	1	2	3	7

Sentences received by 16-20 year old females in Scotland, 1990.

For males, parity between custody and Community Service is only likely for malicious and reckless conduct, and drugs. It would appear, therefore, that Community Service is considered just as appropriate a penalty as custody for females who are convicted for specific kinds of offences.

It is not too fanciful to suggest that, except for fraud, these offences are traditionally male in character. In other words, females charged with 'male' offences have more hope of receiving a Community Service Order than females charged with traditionally female offences. Others may be given custodial sentences because Community Service is not thought to be gender appropriate, based as it is on a punishment, and not a welfare, model. It may therefore be perceived as suitable for those held to be responsible for their actions and not in need of special care and support. Females charged with 'male' crimes may satisfy these conditions, as perhaps may older, married women. What is being suggested here is that the Community Service Order is a heavily genderized penalty, and this bears some responsibility for the number of young adult female offenders receiving custodial sentences in Scotland.

Chaptr Three

Successful Initiatives: Indications of the Way Forward

Over the past few years, the notion that female offenders have been marginalised in the criminal justice system has been reiterated often enough. For the purposes of completing this review, however, marginalisation is an unfortunate metaphor. Because successful initiatives in dealing with female offenders have largely remained undocumented, invisibility and not marginality provides a more accurate description of their problematic location. Primary research is required before any characterisation and analysis of successful initiatives can be made. In the recent past, however, two pieces of original research in England, Wales and Northern Ireland, Carlen's *Alternatives to Women's Imprisonment* (1990) and HM Inspectorate of Probation's *Report on Women Offenders* (1991) have gone some way towards unearthing new initiatives for female offenders-or at least reminding us of their absence.

Why promising measures have remained invisible may be sought in the usual explanations given for women's invisibility in history, as well as some particular to the area. Many initiatives are dependent upon voluntary and short term support, and have been forced to close down just as they are establishing their credibility (Carlen 1990). Many probation- run women's groups are dependent on the interest of particular officers, and survive only as long as they remain in post. Projects most likely to be known outwith their immediate vicinity by reports in the academic and professional journals are usually well funded and long term. Female offender groups are usually neither. Indeed, it was Carlen's own awareness of successful hostels and projects which gave her the impetus to collect information about provision for women offenders, and particularly about what appears to be successful provision. To this effect, questionnaires were sent in the mid 1980s to all Probation Services in England, Wales and Northern Ireland, and many site visits were made. A very similar exercise was undertaken by HM Inspectorate of Probation for England and Wales a few years later (1991). Both publications are readily available and will not be repeated in any detail. For our purposes, two areas of their much wider brief will be highlighted: their analyses of successful accommodation provision and probation-run groups for female offenders. No examples of good Community Service practice for female offenders were offered by either of these reports.

Homelessness is a major cause of incarceration. It is, moreover, an invisible problem, and particularly so for young adult female offenders who are often pressurised into giving their parents' or some other address. Probation and bail hostels for female offenders were found to constitute viable alternatives to imprisonment. Indeed, the Probation Inspectorate found that women bailed to hostels were more likely to receive community disposals, and many custodial sentences could be blamed on the rarity with which recommendations and referrals were made to hostels. This was partly because hostels, and particularly women-only hostels, were themselves scarce in number.

Yet the few existing women-only hostels were not immune from criticism. Their selection procedure is often too heavily resource-led, and many offenders in need of accommodation are rejected because they do not fall into acceptable resource-led criteria. Some women-only hostels are too inflexible in their daily routines so that incarceration, in comparison, seems bearable. For these reasons, hostels restricted to female offenders are sometimes half empty and are therefore perceived to be unnecessary. Yet arguments to the contrary are convincing. A large proportion of female offenders have a history of being abused by men, females are usually in the minority and find the all-male atmosphere of mixed hostels oppressive. Too often, it would appear, women are considered in terms of the needs of the male population and the "civilising effect" which they bring to mixed hostels rather than in terms of how they themselves may benefit. Single-sex hostels, however, are no guarantors of success. Successful hostel initiatives are characterised by their flexibility - both in their selection procedures and in their daily routines.

In their surveys of the probation services of England, Wales and Northern Ireland, the Probation Inspectorate (1991) found that just 18 out of 55 areas in England and Wales had facilities for females which could be offered as alternatives to custody. Carlen (1990) found just 19 out of 57 services in England, Wales and Northern Ireland ran groups specifically for women, (though 3 services reported between 4 and 9 such groups). Yet every one of those services which did run women-only groups claimed an innovative and positive role for them in the rehabilitation of ex-prisoners and the prevention of crime. This was reported to be because of the following:

1. they avert custodial sentences by providing the courts with more options;

2. they intensify the frequency and quality of probation / client contact which is often poor and sporadic when conducted on a one to one basis; and

3. they promote good conduct with the view to eliminating further offences.

Carlen goes on to identify some of the main ways by which groups are successfully able to promote good conduct, as follows:

i. by focusing on offenders' offending behaviour;

ii. by teaching offenders how to deal with stressful situations;

iii. by explaining how the tariff system of sentencing works and the likely consequences of further law-breaking.

(Carlen 1990, p.80)

Because the approach of many women-only probation groups is to focus upon offending behaviour, they also have the additional function of reminding magistrates that women should not be put on probation unless they commit offences which make them liable to a custodial sentence. In other words, they remind magistrates that probation is a high tariff sentence, and that it should be used on the basis of legal criteria and not out of welfare considerations.

Justification for women-only probation groups rests on much the same grounds as women-only hostels. The Probation Inspectorate found that mixed-sex probation groups tend to use female offenders as representatives of their sex, requiring them to cater to the needs of the group rather than to orient to their own needs. The dominance of males in mixed groups offers women little opportunity to develop. Many female offenders were reported to be the victims of child abuse or domestic violence. Finally, women - only groups were reported to help counteract the social isolation which was said to characterise the lives of so many female offenders. Indeed, they were found to be particularly invaluable amongst young adult female offenders by supplementing the gaps in their 'throughcare', as they passed from residential care to isolation, homelessness and crime. In terms of our initial discussion of the social aetiology of criminal behaviour, then, women-only groups prevent recidivism by promoting social affiliations and attachment.

Two recent reports of successful examples of probation-run women's groups draw many of these themes together. Reviewing its service to all offenders in the late 1980s, the Mid-Glamorgan Probation Service began to look afresh at how it might best work with female offenders subject to statutory provision (Jones et al. 1991). It found that courts were sentencing women to probation on welfare rather than offence grounds, probation was doing little to change offending behaviour, and the response of women to probation was either elusive or very demanding in regard to welfare issues. The Probation Service therefore set up a group for high risk female offenders with a structured programme to focus on their offending behaviour, rather than on welfare issues linked with their stereotypical roles. In every aspect of its operation, the group oriented to the offending behaviour of its members, with the following ultimate objectives:

i. to enable women to challenge and confront their behaviour;

ii. to widen their opportunities for alternative behaviour; and

iii. to encourage group members to consider strategies for dealing with their perceived powerlessness in changing their behaviour.

In other words, the group sought to change the model of 'man' by which the offending behaviour of women is usually understood. Seeing women as offenders and as responsible for their actions, and not as victims of circumstance, was understood to change the language that reinforces helplessness. Indeed, one of the main indicators of the success of the probation group was that it heightened awareness amongst women of their offending behaviour. This made possible more meaningful individual supervision sessions with probation officers. The support of middle management was also reported to be essential for the effectiveness of new programmes. The receptivity of magistrates to new initiatives for female offenders, for example, was believed to be highly dependent upon good inter-agency communication and collaboration. The importance of inter-agency work for the successful implementation of new initiatives has already been well documented in our initial report.

The second case study was set up by the Avon Probation Service in the recognition that though female offenders were far likelier to receive probation than male offenders, provision for females had largely been limited to one-to-one individualised responses (Mistry 1989). Even what were ostensibly "groups" for female offenders were found to be little more than extensions of one-to-one work. Clients were being "social worked", facilities were poor and the welfare model predominated. A women-only group was therefore set up with the aim of helping female offenders to understand their own offending behaviour and to take some control over their lives. Too often, it was felt, women in 'mixed' groups only served to help men understand their own offending behaviour.

Over the past six years, more than 120 women, mainly between 18 and 25, and 65% of them single parents, have gone through the group. An independent study found the women felt more supported by the group than in one-to-one settings with probation officers, and that 90% of the women had completed their probation orders without further convictions. The scheme constituted a success for the courts and the probation service, and not just because of low re-offending rates. It demonstrated that attendance need not be problematic if the needs of clients are being met. Regular referrals from probation teams over these years confirmed that single sex groups within the structure of a probation order are a viable method of supervising female offenders. Because of the success of the original group, a number of others have been set up in the Avon area.

Concluding Remarks

Part 2 has attempted to draw females into our initial review of criminal justice and related services for young adult offenders. Few conclusions and even less recommendations can be made at this point, and there will be no attempt to conform to protocol by doing so. Instead, we will begin by urging for what is traditionally left to last - the need for further research.

In many ways, this has been a particularly frustrating term of research because the method of investigation has been limited by more than the usual constraints of time and other resources. Had it proceeded no further than the literature review, then some coherence to the findings might have given cause for satisfaction. As it was, the statistical data only raised more questions about what is happening in Scotland than the literature ever asked. Because the data are open to many interpretations, the need to supplement their examination with interviewing, observation and documentary analysis soon became apparent. In informal conversations, for example, the reasons given for why so few 16 and 17 years old female offenders were under Community Service Orders and why so many, by comparison, were in custody, were as various as the positions in the criminal justice system which these informants held.

At a time when social work departments in Scotland are re-organising to give offenders specialist and quality service, it seems a most crucial and opportune time to ask:

1. What provisions are now being made for female offenders ?

2. What deficiencies in the criminal justice system and related services for female offenders should now be brought to the attention of policy makers?

The report recently produced by HM Inspectorate of Probation for England and Wales comes immediately to mind as a model for investigating these questions. A retrospective study tracing the paths by which young female offenders are received into custody may usefully pinpoint where the deficiencies in the system(s) lie. This should be complemented by a Scotland-wide survey to collate information on what provisions are presently available for female offenders and what needs should now be addressed.

In the introduction, some concern over the way women were being added into the research agenda was raised. Long term development of the field requires that the study of gender issues means more than simply "adding in" women. It requires

96

some re-drawing of the picture. In this report, there has been some focus on the related discourses of chivalry and welfare, and how their employment in the criminal justice system and adjunct services appears to have detrimental consequences for young adult females. Their absence in relation to the management of young adult male offenders may be as much a cause for concern as their presence is for females.

References and Bibliography

Allen, H. (1987)
Justice Unbalanced, Milton Keynes, Open University Press.

Bottoms, A. (1990)
Intermediate Treatment and Juvenile Justice: Key Findings and Implications, London, HMSO.

Bottoms, A. and McWilliams, W.
"A non-treatment paradigm for probation practice", (1979) *British Journal of Social Work, 9 (2)* , 159-202.

Braithwaite, J. (1989)
Crime, Shame and Reintegration, Cambridge, Cambridge University Press.

Carlen, P. (1983)
Women's Imprisonment, London, outledge and Kegan Paul.

Carlen, P. (1988)
Women, Crime and Poverty, Milton Keynes, Open University Press.

Carlen, P. (1990)
Alternatives to Women's Imprisonment, Milton Keynes, Open University Press.

Casale, S. (1989)
Women Inside, London, Civil Liberties Trust.

Casburn, M. (1979)
Girls Will Be Girls, London, Women Research and Resources Centre.

Datesman, S. and Scarpitti, F.
Women, Crime and Justice, New York, OUP. (eds) (1980)

Eaton, M. (1986)
Justice for Women, Milton Keynes, Open University Press.

Farrington, D. and Bennett, T.
"Police Cautioning of Juveniles in London", *(1989) British Journal of Criminology, 23 (3).*

Farrington, D. and Morris, A. (1983)
'Sex, sentencing and conviction', *Journal of Criminology, 23(3)*: 229-48.

Gelsthorpe, L. (1985)
Gender Issues in Juvenile Justice; An Annotated Bibliography, Lancaster, Information Systems.

Genders, E. and Players, N.(1989) "Women in prison: the treatment, the control and the experience", in Carlen, P. and Worrall, A. (eds) *Gender, Crime and Justice*, Milton Keynes, Open University Press.

Hedderman, C. (1990) "The effects of defendants' demeanour on sentencing in magistrates courts", *Research Bulletin No. 29*, London, RPU Home Office.

Heidensohn, F. (1985) *Women and Crime,* London: Macmillan.

Hirschi, T. (1969) *The Causes of Delinquency*, Berkeley: University of California Press.

HM Inspectorate of Probation. *Report on Women Offenders and Probation* (1991) *Service Provision.*

Jackson, H. and Smith, L.(1987) "Female offenders: an analysis of Social Inquiry Reports", *Research Bulletin No.23*, London:, RPU Home Office.

Jones, M. et al (1991) "The Miskin model of groupwork with women offenders", *Groupwork, 4(3):*, 215-30.

Klein, D. (1976) "The etiology of female crime: a review of the literature" in Datesman and Scarpitti (eds) *ibid.*

Martinson, R. (1982) "What works? Questions and answers about prison reform", *Public Interest, 35*, 22-54.

Mayhew, P. et al. (1989) *The 1988 British Crime Survey,* London, HMSO.

McWilliams, W. (ed.) (1981) *Community Service By Order*, Edinburgh, Scottish Academic Press.

Mistry, T. (1989) "Establishing a feminist model of groupwork in the probation service", *Groupwork, 2(2)*, 145-58.

Morris, A. and Gelsthorpe, L.(eds.) *Women and Crime*, Cambridge Institute of 1981) Criminology.

Morris, A. and Wilkinson, C. "Just an easy answer", *Community Care*, Dec. 8th. (1983)

Morris, A. (1987) *Women, Crime and Criminal Justice*, Oxford, Blackwell.

NACRO, (1988)   "Women, cautioning and sentencing", *NACRO Briefing,* London, NACRO.

NACRO, (1989)   "Women and criminal justice", *NACRO Briefing,* London, NACRO.

NACRO, (1990)   "The Home Office Circular on the cautioning of offenders: Implications for juvenile justice", *Juvenile Crime Section,* London, NACRO.

Nagel, I. (1981)   "Sex Differences in the Processing of Criminal Defendants", in Morris and Gelsthorpe, *ibid.*

National Youth Agency (1992)   Personal Communication.

Parker, H. et al. (1981)   *Receiving Juvenile Justice,* Oxford, Blackwell.

Pollak, O. (1950)   *The Criminality of Women,* Philadelphia, University of Pennsylvania Press.

Scottish Office (1990)   *Community Service Bulletin.*
       (1991)   *Children and Crime, Scotland 1989.*
       (1991)   *Criminal Proceedings in Scottish Courts, 1989.*
       (1992)   *Prison Statistics, Scotland 1990.*
       (1992)   *Community Service Bulletin.*

Seear, N. and Player, E. (1986)   *Women in the Penal System,* London, Howard League for Penal Reform.

Stedward, G. and Millar, A.(1989)   *Diversion From Prosecution: Vol.I . Diversion to Social Work,* Edinburgh, CRU (Scottish Office).

Thomas, W.I. (1907)   *Sex and Society ,* Boston, Little Brown.

Webb, D. (1984)   "More on gender and justice: girl offenders on supervision", *Sociology, 18(3).*

Worrall, A.(1981)   "Out of place: female offenders in court", *Probation Journal , 28 (3),* 90-3.

Worrall, A. (1990)   *Offending Women,* London, Routledge.

Printed in the UK for HMSO Scotland
CCNo 20249 8C 7/94